BRITAIN IN OLD  S

MANCHESTER

CHRIS E. MAKEPEACE

SUTTON PUBLISHING LIMITED

Sutton Publishing Limited
Phoenix Mill · Thrupp · Stroud
Gloucestershire · GL5 2BU

First published 1996

Copyright © Chris E. Makepeace, 1996

Cover photographs: *front*: a street trader selling
'lucky white heather' in Market Street; *back*:
Princess Aviaries, a 'livestock emporium' in
central Manchester.

British Library Cataloguing in Publication Data
A catalogue record for this book is available from the
British Library.

ISBN 0-7509-1204-9

Typeset in 10/12 Perpetua.
Typesetting and origination by
Sutton Publishing Limited.
Printed in Great Britain by
Ebenezer Baylis, Worcester

CONTENTS

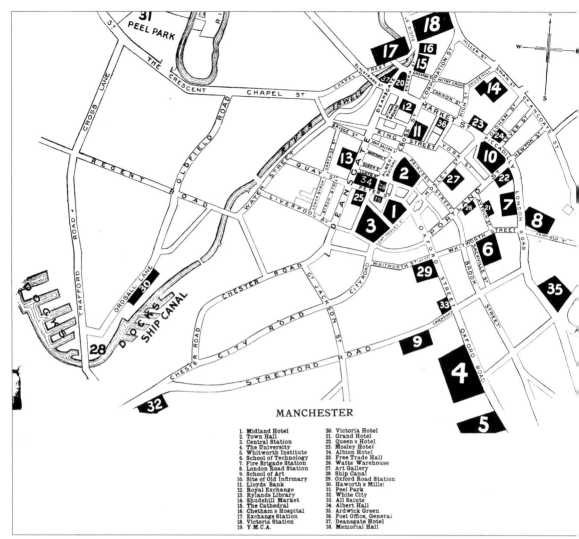

MANCHESTER

1. Midland Hotel
2. Town Hall
3. Central Station
4. The University
5. Whitworth Institute
6. School of Technology
7. Fire Brigade Station
8. London Road Station
9. School of Art
10. Site of Old Infirmary
11. Lloyds' Bank
12. Royal Exchange
13. Rylands Library
14. Shudehill Market
15. The Cathedral
16. Chetham's Hospital
17. Exchange Station
18. Victoria Station
19. Y.M.C.A.
20. Victoria Hotel
21. Grand Hotel
22. Queen's Hotel
23. Mosley Hotel
24. Albion Hotel
25. Free Trade Hall
26. Watts Warehouse
27. Art Gallery
28. Ship Canal
29. Oxford Road Station
30. Haworth's Mills
31. Peel Park
32. White City
33. All Saints
34. Albert Hall
35. Ardwick Green
36. Post Office, General
37. Deansgate Hotel
38. Memorial Hall

This map of Manchester was published in about 1905 and shows the main roads and public buildings in the centre of the city. The main street pattern shown here has changed little over the past ninety years, although some of the roads have now been pedestrianized and many of the small courts and streets, which lay between Market Street and Shudehill, have disappeared either as a result of the blitz or post-war redevelopment. Many of the buildings shown on this map are still standing today although in some cases they have been found new uses or have been refurbished.

INTRODUCTION

When Angus Bethune Reach visited Manchester in 1849, he described the town as 'Queen of the Cotton cities . . . this great capital of the weavers and spinners of the earth, the Manchester of the power-loom, the Manchester of the League, our Manchester – is but a thing of yesterday . . . considerably within two-thirds of a century the scattered villages of Manchester, Salford, Hulme, Pendleton, Chorlton and two or three others, became the vast cotton metropolis which has lately succeeded in swaying the industrial and commercial policy of England.' Twelve months earlier the editor of the *Builder* had commented that 'Manchester has been pointed to as the type of one grand idea – Machinery – an idea which belongs to our own age exclusively, and is full of great results hardly yet foreshadowed.' These two comments sum up Manchester's growth to the mid-nineteenth century, namely that it was a product of recent developments. Between 1751 and 1851 the population of central Manchester had risen from around 17,000 to over 186,000, after which it started to decline although, as a result of absorbing the surrounding districts, the total population of the city continued to rise until the 1930s, peaking at around 737,000 just before the Second World War.

Although Manchester developed rapidly between 1750 and 1850, the period often described as that of the Industrial Revolution, the origins of Manchester can be traced back to the Roman occupation of Britain in the first century AD. Around AD 79 the Romans established a small fort on a sandstone buff, overlooking the confluence of the rivers Irwell and Medlock. In the beginning the fort consisted of an earthen rampart with a wooden stockade at the top and protected by a double line of ditches. The fort was rebuilt on several occasions, the last time being about AD 200 when stone replaced the wood. Outside the walls a small civilian settlement developed which included metal working facilities as well as the usual type of buildings one associates with a garrison – inns, shops, temples and a bath-house. Radiating from the fort were a number of roads, the most important of which was that from Chester to York. Other roads led to places like Melandra (near Glossop), Ribchester, Castleshaw (above Oldham) and Coccium (believed to be Wigan).

After the Romans left in about AD 410 little is known about what happened in Manchester. Place name evidence suggests that there was both Saxon and Danish influence, but archaeological evidence is non-existent. There is a brief reference to Manchester in the Anglo-Saxon Chronicle for 919, but its full meaning and what King Edward did in Manchester is not clear. The only certainty during this period is that the settlement migrated from around the fort to another defendable site overlooking the confluence of the rivers Irwell and Irk. Even in the Domesday Book there is only the briefest of references to Manchester. It indicates that Manchester was within the Hundred of Salford, that King Edward was Lord of the Manor of Salford (implying that the manor of Manchester was subordinate to the manor of Salford), that there was a parish church in Manchester dedicated to St Mary, and that the church held certain lands free from all taxes except the geld.

Medieval Manchester was not a large settlement. It was centred around the residence of the lords of the manor, now Chetham's School, the parish church, now the cathedral, and the market-place, with the main roads being Deansgate, Old Millgate, Long Millgate, Withy Grove and a small section of Market Street. The importance of the town as a centre is illustrated by the grant of an annual fair in 1222 and the attempt in 1301 to grant it a charter. Although the charter was rescinded in 1359 it established a pattern of local government for Manchester which continued to operate until 1792, when the first police commissioners were appointed. After this the Court Leet continued to operate in tandem with them until the borough council was elected in 1838. The Court Leet was finally abolished in 1845 after the council had paid the Mosley family £250,000 for the manorial rights. There is also evidence that from the late thirteenth century there were people in Manchester who earned their living not from farming but by trading, and had shops in the town.

Although Manchester was not a borough it was a market town and the centre of an extensive medieval parish, which covered most of modern Manchester as well as part of Salford and several surrounding areas. In 1421 Thomas de la Warre, who was not only the lord of the manor but also a priest, secured for the church a charter which established a college of clergy to provide for the spiritual needs of the people of the parish. In addition he gave the church his manor house as a home for the clergy, buildings which are now part of Chetham's School. The charter, although suspended from time to time, remained in operation until 1847 when the Diocese of Manchester was created and the collegiate church became Manchester Cathedral.

By the sixteenth century Manchester was also becoming the leading town in south-east Lancashire. Much of its wealth was generated from the woollen trade, there being a number of wealthy woollen merchants in Manchester at that time. The wool appears to have been imported from Ireland and distributed to local people to turn into cloth, who then returned it to the merchants who took it to London to sell. One of the wealthiest of these clothiers, or cloth merchants, was Humphrey Chetham, whose funeral when he died in 1653 cost over £1,200, while another merchant family, the Mosleys, purchased the Manor of Manchester in 1596.

During the Civil War Manchester supported the Parliamentary forces and was even besieged for a short while in 1642. However, like other areas, it welcomed the restoration of Charles II, the conduit in the market-place flowing with claret on the day of his coronation. The accession of William and Mary in 1689 resulted in the establishment of the first Nonconformist chapel in the town and the erection of St Ann's Church to cater for those who did not agree with the High Church, pro-Jacobite views expressed at the collegiate church. The division of Manchester into two factions became apparent in 1715 when a mob supporting the Old Pretender attacked and seriously damaged Cross Street Chapel, and again in 1745 when many of the supporters of the Hanoverians left the town before Bonnie Prince Charlie arrived. The High Church faction tended to see the Low Church faction and Nonconformists as allies, so when proposals were made in the early eighteenth century for a workhouse to be governed by a body drawn equally from the three groups they opposed it, presumably because they thought they would be in a permanent minority. The same applied when proposals were made for a borough charter shortly afterwards.

In many respects 1745 marks the end of a period in Manchester's history. Up to then Manchester was a market town and a regional centre, but as the eighteenth century progressed Manchester's importance began to increase dramatically helped by developments affecting the textile industry. During the eighteenth century cotton began to replace wool as the main component of cloth which was manufactured in the area. At the same time developments took place which resulted in the weaving of broad cloth, using the flying shuttle, which upset the balance between spinning and weaving. The flying shuttle was still capable of being used domestically, but the machines required to speed up yarn production required water power. Both Arkwright's water-frame and Crompton's mule operated more efficiently with a mechanical means of power, and in the case of the mule far more efficiently with steam power as its size could be increased to over 1,000 spindles. Initially water was used, but from the 1790s steam power came to be used to drive machines. It was with the development of a rotative motion enabling steam engines to drive machines that Manchester began to expand very rapidly. Manchester was ideally situated to take advantage of the new form of power. Land on the edge of the town was relatively cheap, it was flat and there was cheap bulk transportation available not only to bring the raw cotton from Liverpool and take the finished products away, but also to bring coal in to produce the steam. A further factor was the presence of a large labour force which was growing at an amazing rate in the 1790s and early 1800s. People were coming into Manchester seeking work. New housing was required, which in itself created employment as well as the very poor housing conditions made famous by people like J.P. Kay and Frederick Engels.

The first cotton mills were built in Chorton-on-Medlock and Ancoats in the 1790s, their six to seven storeys overshadowing the houses. For the first time, people began to be ruled not by hours of daylight and their own free will but by the factory hooter or bell. When these early mills opened they relied on natural light, but after 1805 gas lighting was gradually introduced which allowed employees to work longer and longer hours. For the first time it was possible to see the conditions under which people lived and worked and the consequences of poor housing and long hours for men, women and children. This may have encouraged observers to begin to collect statistical information not only on working conditions but also on disease and living conditions, and to publish the results of their findings. Two of Manchester's leading societies in this field were the Manchester Statistical Society, founded in 1833 and the Manchester and Salford Sanitary Association, formed in 1851.

As well as manufacturing cotton Manchester was also the centre of the cotton trade. The Royal Exchange was where manufacturers and others met to exchange commercial information and strike deals. At the same time firms with mills outside Manchester established warehouses where customers could see the company's products, one of the best known of which was that of the Rylands company. Other warehouses were developed by wholesalers who sold not only the cloth, but also the goods made from the cloth, firms like J. & N. Philips and J. & S. Watts. All these firms were connected in some way with the cotton industry, which it was said made for the home market before breakfast and for export for the rest of the day'. At the same time as Manchester developed as the centre of the cotton industry there began to develop various financial facilities such as banking and insurance. These were essential for the smooth running of an increasingly complex business life in the city.

The demands of the cotton industry had an effect on the industrial base of Manchester and surrounding districts. Gradually the demand for a wider range of colours that did not wash out led to developments in the bleaching and dyeing industries, which in turn put pressure on the chemists to develop synthetic colours. To produce these the chemical industry began to develop using, at first, the by-products of the gas industry. The knock-on effect of the demands of the cotton industry were enormous.

The use of steam to drive machines also affected industry in the area. As machines went faster so wood was replaced by metal. No longer was it possible to adapt a part if it did not fit; parts had to be accurately made. This gave rise to new machines that reproduced the same part accurately many times over, and later machines developed to make these machines. Gradually the skilled workman was able to be replaced by a semi-skilled man and ultimately by a man whose job it was merely to operate the machine. Manchester developed an engineering industry of its own. Developing from the manufacture of textile machines, engineers began to make machine tools which encouraged others to produce large products such as bridges, railway engines and, in this century, motor cars and aircraft.

In order for the technological developments to have their full effect other developments in transportation were essential. The opening of the Bridgewater Canal in 1764 provided Manchester with a means of bulk transport which was relatively cheap and efficient. When the canal was extended to Liverpool in 1777 raw cotton and finished products could be imported and exported easily. The canal network could also be used to carry coal to the mills as well as building materials and, very importantly, food. Until a cheap means of bulk transport had been developed the size of towns had been limited by the amount of food that could be grown and transported into the town. With canals there came the opportunity to draw on the rich agricultural areas of north Cheshire and south Lancashire. Thus it was possible to feed 70,000 people without the risk of riots.

The nineteenth century saw further changes in transport with the development of railways. Manchester became the centre of a railway network stretching throughout the country. Not only were people carried, but increasingly freight became the largest revenue earner. However, as the railways took over the canals there were complaints about the rising cost of transport to and from Liverpool. This ultimately led to the movement which resulted in the building of the Manchester Ship Canal between 1887 and 1893. It was Mancunians who lead the movement and who played a leading role in the battle to secure Parliamentary approval between 1882 and 1885, and it was Manchester City Council that came to the company's rescue in the early 1890s when funding became difficult. When the Manchester ship canal was opened the dream of linking Manchester directly to the sea came true. More recently international travel has been fostered by the development of Manchester International Airport for both freight and passenger services. In many respects, this is a continuation of the transport changes started back in the eighteenth century which helped Manchester become a major city.

When Manchester became a borough in 1838 it was not without its opponents, who felt that the existing system of local government was adequate. The new borough council inherited a town with few regulations and many problems. The council, however, was prepared to tackle some of these, but it was a slow process. The passing of the 1844 Police Act was the first of many attempts to try to improve conditions in the town. Likewise the decision to obtain water from outside the town's boundaries was revolutionary, but essential if conditions were to improve. It should be noted that the police commissioners were not slow at seizing a chance if one arose, as is well illustrated by the decision in 1817 to sell gas to the public, although they did not have permission or the authority to do so. The borough council took the opportunity to supply the surrounding areas with gas, water and electricity. This provision of an infrastructure for the surrounding districts gradually bound them to the city and made their take-over a lot easier at the end of the nineteenth and in the early years of the twentieth century.

Over the last two centuries there have been many developments in which Manchester has played a leading part. Technological developments have helped industry develop, but also there is the important field of 'ideas'. The Manchester Literary and Philosophical Society provided a forum which brought together scientists, technologists and engineers while the trading connection encouraged the growth of the free trade movement in the mid-nineteenth century.

It is said that from 'little acorns big oaks grow'; in the case of Manchester, from the small Roman fort of AD 79 and the associated civilian settlement so the great city of Manchester developed, although it was over 1,700 years before the town became one of the country's leading settlements with a commercial and economic influence which was enormous. It has been said that Manchester liked to call itself 'the second city of the Empire'. Manchester was, and still is, justly proud of its achievements especially over the last 250 years. Reach was right when he described the town as 'Queen of the Cotton cities' while the editors of the volume published for the visit of the British Association in 1962 called Manchester 'The centre of a region'. Manchester may not be large in terms of population, but its conurbation and its influence covers very large area indeed. It may still be true that 'What Manchester thinks today, the rest of the country thinks tomorrow.'

STREET SCENES

The main streets of any thriving town are bustling and full of life. Manchester in the late nineteenth and early twentieth century was no exception to this with people hurrying about their daily business. De Tocqueville commented in 1835 that 'crowds are ever in a hurry . . . their footsteps are brisk, their looks preoccupied . . .'. Fourteen years later, A. B. Reach, writing for the *Morning Chronicle*, described the main streets as 'busy and swarming . . . crowded at once with the evidences of wealth and commerce . . . crowds of busy pedestrians of every class . . . bustling from counting-house to counting-house, and bank to bank . . .'. These descriptions of Manchester's streets would have been applicable in the twentieth century as much as in the nineteenth century.

The photographs in this section take the reader on a tour of central Manchester from Piccadilly along Portland Street, Oxford Street, St Peter's Square, Mosley Street, Albert Square, Peter Street, Deansgate, the Market Place and Market Street back to Piccadilly. Many changes have taken place in the buildings which line these street, changes brought about by the blitz and redevelopment with further changes being made as a result of the 1996 IRA terrorist bomb. For a city to be alive changes have to take place. Old buildings will have to be replaced, although the extent of the changes will depend on the type of buildings involved and the potential for finding suitable new uses for them when their original use has become obsolete.

One important change that has occurred since many of these photographs were taken is the change from horse-drawn vehicles to vehicles powered by the internal combustion engine. Congestion existed in the nineteenth century just as it does in the late twentieth century and complaints were made about the danger of crossing roads. Attempts are being made to remove traffic from the centre of Manchester with pedestrianization schemes like those for King Street, St Ann's Square and Market Street. One result of pedestrianization is that it is now possible to stand back and look at the upper floors of buildings without the fear of stepping backwards into a moving vehicle. Often it is the upper floors of buildings which reveal interesting details, such as dates of construction, the name of the building and even initials of the owner or builder.

Photographs of street scenes paint a far more vivid picture of the town than a large number of words. From a photograph it is possible to gain an impression of the buildings, which building stood next to which and even who occupied various shops. As well as what the buildings looked like, photographs can also be used to show the type of vehicles which used the street, the posters which appeared on walls, the dress of the people and even the street furniture. The more street scenes are examined, the more detail can be discovered, especially if the illustrations are used in conjunction with other sources such as directories and newspapers.

Photographs of street scenes come from many sources — some have been taken by individuals, others by official bodies and yet others have been transformed into postcards. Fortunately, many of the postcards of central Manchester show busy streets rather than just buildings and so they are more lively than they might otherwise be.

It is to be hoped that this section on the streets of central Manchester will enable the reader to build up a picture of the town before the blitz and post-war reconstruction and redevelopment.

Until the late eighteenth century Piccadilly, or Lever's Row as it was then known, marked the southern extent of Manchester. In 1812 Lever's Row was renamed Piccadilly, a name which was already in use for the section between Newton Street and what is now the approach to Piccadilly station. Originally Piccadilly was lined with private houses, some of whose occupants were associated with the Infirmary, which dominated the area and stood where Piccadilly Gardens are now sited. During the nineteenth century the houses were replaced by hotels, shops and offices, although one still survives between Lever Street and Newton Street to show what the original buildings must have looked like. This particular illustration was taken towards the end of the nineteenth century, looking south from where Royal Buildings are now situated. On the extreme left is the Albion Hotel, which, according to a French visitor, had one of the best cuisines in Europe in the mid-nineteenth century. The Albion Hotel closed in 1926 and was replaced by Woolworth's store. On the extreme right is the Queen's Hotel, which was originally a series of town houses. The Queen's Hotel was well known in the late nineteenth century for its turtle soup, which was sold in a condensed form to other hotels and for important occasions. The hotels which were found in and around Piccadilly had a large number of guests from various parts of the United Kingdom as well as from abroad. Many were businessmen who had come to do business with Manchester's firms, but also a number of people who could be described as tourists stayed in them as well.

For over 150 years Piccadilly was dominated by the Manchester Royal Infirmary, on the left of the picture. The original Infirmary building was little more than a very large Georgian house with a wing fronting on to Portland Street. Shortly after it was completed, another wing was added facing Mosley Street. Gradually other alterations were made which resulted in the masking of the original Georgian building. By the third quarter of the nineteenth century discussions were being held about the possibility of the Infirmary moving to a new site where it would be able to expand. At the same time, concern was beginning to be expressed about the sanitary state of the building and the cost of putting things right. In 1902 the decision was taken to move the hospital to a 'green-field' site in Chorlton-on-Medlock, close to the eye hospital. The decision was made in the light of new developments in the field of medicine, such as the arrival of the X-ray and the fact that bed occupancy rates showed that almost every day of the year there were only a few empty beds. The new hospital was completed in 1908 and the patients were moved in December that year. This photograph was taken in 1908 just before the Infirmary closed. In front of the Infirmary is the Esplanade, which was created in 1853 when the ponds and fountains were filled in and the area paved over and statues added.

Even before the Infirmary had moved to its new premises the debate about what the site in Piccadilly should be used for was opened. Various suggestions were made including a new Royal Exchange and a new art galley. The issue was debated at council meetings and in the columns of the local papers, but there was general agreement that the old buildings should be demolished. Work started early in 1910 and by April only the front portico remained. This spectacular photograph was taken in April 1910 when the columns which graced the front façade of the building were demolished.

With the demolition of the old Infirmary an open space was created in the centre of one of the busiest parts of Manchester. Before any use could be agreed, the city council was faced with the problem of finding a new home for the Free Reference Library as their existing premises had been declared unsafe. As a temporary measure huts were erected to house the library, but the final decision on where it should go and what should happen to the old Infirmary site was delayed by the outbreak of war in August 1914. The site had already been landscaped as a temporary measure and this was retained after the war, providing an important open space in this part of Manchester. This picture, taken in about 1927, shows Piccadilly Gardens, while in the background is Browns warehouse, designed by Edward Walters, the façade of which is now the Portland Hotel. The warehouse on the extreme right was demolished in the early 1970s, its replacement office block becoming the offices of the now abolished Greater Manchester County Council in 1975.

To many people Piccadilly is regarded as the centre of Manchester. This photograph shows one of the hotels which was to be found in the area, the White Bear. This building had originally been the town house of the Lever family of Alkrington, but had been sold in about 1772 and converted into a coaching inn. Although the front was altered on several occasions, when the building was demolished in about 1906 some of the original structure of the building was discovered at the rear. To the right of the White Bear is the Mosley Hotel, which had moved from Market Street to Piccadilly in 1828, when its original location was required for road improvements. In the 1890s the hotel was rebuilt with many improved facilities. The Mosley Hotel closed after the First World War and the building was replaced by the Piccadilly Cinema.

As pedestrians walk along the Esplanade at Piccadilly, they pass several statues erected in the nineteenth century. The one shown in this photograph is of the Duke of Wellington, which was unveiled in 1856. The statue, sculpted by Matthew Noble and unveiled before a crowd of 100,000, represented Wellington not as a military leader but as a parliamentary statesman, a decision which did not meet with universal approval. However, a concession was made to Wellington's military career by including a pile of dispatches at his feet and two panels depicting the Battle of Waterloo and the Battle of Assaye in India.

The first modern warehouse was erected by Richard Cobden, to the designs of Edward Walters, on Mosley Street in about 1838. Twenty years later what has been described as the most magnificent of Manchester's cotton warehouses was completed for the firm of S. & J. Watts on Portland Street. The building was designed by Travis and Magnall and cost almost £100,000. The design was said to have included four different styles of Renaissance architecture. At the end of the nineteenth century S. & J. Watts employed over 1,000 people, and claimed that all orders received in the morning post were dispatched that same day. In the 1970s the building closed as a warehouse, and after several scares about its future was converted into a hotel.

Until the late nineteenth century Portland Street ended where it met David Street (later Princess Street). Beyond the junction there were canal wharves from the Rochdale Canal, including a site occupied by Pickfords. The buildings closest to the junction of Portland Street and Princess Street were erected in the early nineteenth century although several were modernized in the late nineteenth century. For instance, the building with a gable was re-fronted in about 1883 for Armstrong's, who were stationers. It is interesting to note the advertisements on the gable wall, which indicate the kind of things the public were being encouraged to buy in the early years of the twentieth century. The junction here was always very busy, hence the policeman in the centre of the road directing traffic.

In 1890 the Refuge Assurance Company decided to build its own offices on a site which had recently become available at the junction of Whitworth Street and Oxford Street, as the rented premises they occupied had become overcrowded. Alfred Waterhouse was chosen to design the new offices. He presented his plans for a six-storey building in January 1891, and the work was completed and the offices ready for occupation by mid-summer 1895. Within a decade these new offices had also been filled and so Paul Waterhouse, the son of Alfred, was commissioned to design an extension, which was completed in 1912. To link the two blocks the clock tower was constructed; it became a landmark in this part of Manchester. A further extension was added in the 1930s. When the Refuge Assurance Co. moved to Wilmslow at the end of the 1980s their former offices were converted into a hotel, now called the Palace, which has retained the late Victorian and Edwardian splendour of large open plan offices. This view, taken just before the First World War, shows the clock tower from the entrance to Oxford Road station.

This view is of the corner of Whitworth Street West and Oxford Street and was taken from the approach to Oxford Road station. On the left is St Mary's Hospital, which was opened in 1892 as a replacement for an overcrowded building on Quay Street. Shortly after the hospital was opened St Mary's merged with the Southern Hospital for Women and Children, and a new building was erected on High Street in Chorlton-on-Medlock. The central Manchester building continued to be used until the 1960s, when it was closed and eventually demolished. On the extreme right is the Palace Theatre, opened in 1891 and refurbished in about 1912. The white building in the centre is the St James building, which was completed in about 1912 by the Calico Printers Association. It was named after the St James Theatre and Hall which stood on the site from about 1880 until 1909. The St James Theatre was said to the home of 'heavy drama' while it was at the St James Hall that the Tiller girls first went through the routines that were to make them so famous in the twentieth century.

The construction of Oxford Street started in 1790 with the intention of linking central Manchester with the Manchester to Wilmslow Turnpike Road, which passed through villages like Withington and Didsbury. When the new road was constructed the River Tib, which flowed around the southern side of St Peter's Square, had to be culverted. Gradually Oxford Road became lined with buildings, but it was not until the late nineteenth century that the part nearest the River Medlock and the southern boundary of the Manchester township was developed, as the eastern side of the road consisted mainly of canal wharves associated with the Rochdale Canal. There were, however, a few factories and mills close to the canal at this point. On the opposite side of Oxford Street were the works of Sharp Stewart and Co., who made textile machinery as well as railway locomotives. This view shows the junction of St Peter's Square and Oxford Street, probably in about 1910. The buildings on the right, which included the Princes Theatre, were demolished after the Second World War and were replaced by Peter House. In 1905 the buildings on the right hand side were occupied by a cocoa merchant, a cricketers' outfitters and a boot maker, while the offices included several merchants and a maker-up of cotton goods. On the opposite side of the road at the same time was a branch of Boots, a portmanteau manufacturer, a fruiterer and the well-known Princes' Cafe, founded by a Mr Tamvaca in 1870.

If you follow the buildings on the left of the previous photograph into St Peter's Square, the buildings shown in this particular illustration would have been seen. This photograph was taken in about 1929. The buildings on the corner, of which only part can be seen, were known as St Peter's Chambers and were occupied mainly by surgeons, while next door was Duncan & Foster Ltd, caterers. The tall building was a mixture of shops at street level and offices on the upper floors. In 1931 the shops included a tailor, a hairdresser, a wallpaper dealer and a gramophone dealer and musical instrument seller. The upper floors were mainly occupied by firms associated with the textile industry. All the buildings were demolished in the early 1970s and replaced by Elisabeth House.

On the corner of St Peter's Square and Peter Street stood an impressive block of buildings which were erected in the 1860s and 1870s to replace what was described as 'a motley collection of buildings'. Although they have the appearance of town houses, they were in fact designed to be offices. When this photograph was taken at the beginning of the twentieth century, these buildings included a café, a tailor, professional offices and one property, No. 3, which provided offices for doctors. These buildings were demolished in 1928 when work started on the construction of the new central library.

When the Manchester Reference Library was forced to move from its premises in the former Town Hall at the corner of Cross Street and King Street in 1912, it had to move into temporary accommodation in Piccadilly. Plans to erect a new central library were delayed by the First World War so it was not until the early 1920s that the city council could once more start to plan for a new library. A site was chosen at the corner of St Peter's Square and Peter Street, and Vincent Harris was selected to design the new building. Work started in 1929 with the foundation stone being laid in 1930 by Ramsay MacDonald, the prime minister. Gradually the steel frame of the library rose above the surrounding area as this photograph shows. The structure of the dome and the central circular reading room can also been seen. The library was completed in 1934 at a cost of £413,000, and was officially opened by George V, who also laid the foundation of the Town Hall Extension, also designed by Vincent Harris, on a site between the library and the existing Town Hall.

St Peter's Square was linked to Piccadilly by Mosley Street, named after the Mosley family who were lords of the manor of Manchester from 1596 to 1845. Originally many of the buildings which were erected on Mosley Street were private houses although many had warehouses and workshops at the rear. There were a few public buildings to be seen, such as the Portico Library, the Manchester Assembly Rooms and Mosley Street Independent Chapel. In 1823 the Royal Manchester Institution was formed with the aim of trying to encourage Mancunians to appreciate the fine arts such as painting and sculpture. Charles Barry was commissioned to design a suitable building for the collection of paintings and sculptures which it was hoped would be collected. Work on the new art gallery started in 1825 and was completed by 1834. In 1882 the Art Gallery, together with its collections, was passed to Manchester City Council, who still own the building and the collections. This view shows the Art Gallery with the Union Club, established in 1825, in the background. The building housing the Union Club was designed by Richard Lane and completed in 1835.

This photograph of the junction of Mosley Street and York Street in about 1910 clearly illustrates the problems Manchester had with traffic congestion in the early twentieth century, with lorries carrying goods to and from warehouses mingling with trams and a large number of pedestrians trying to cross the road. In the background is Colwyn Chambers, completed in about 1892.

In the late eighteenth century a number of societies were formed in different parts of the country to bring together men who had a common interest in science and technology. In 1781 the Manchester Literary and Philosophical Society was founded by twenty-four men, many of whom were medical men at the infirmary. Initially the Society met at Cross Street Chapel, but in 1799 it moved to its own building on George Street. The membership included many of the leading scientists of the period. Among the earliest members were the Henrys and John Dalton, whose work on colour blindness and whose atomic theory were revolutionary. Other important scientists who were members included J.P. Joule, Edward Frankland, Henry Roscoe and Carl Schorlemmer. Other members included William Fairbairn, an engineer, J. B. Dancer, manufacturer of scientific instruments and James Mudd, photographer. The Society provided a meeting place for scientists and engineers to exchange ideas on the latest developments. Their building was damaged in the Christmas blitz of 1940, which resulted in the loss of important historic scientific papers. This photograph shows the Society's house in the early twentieth century.

The Literary and Philosophical Society not only had an ordinary membership, but also a number of honorary members, who were usually prominent scientists of the day. Among those who were given this honour were Bunsen, developer of the Bunsen burner, Neils Bohr, J. J. Berzelius, who put Dalton's atomic theory on a firm experimental basis, and D. I. Mendeleev, pictured here in the centre of the front row. Mendeleev was responsible for the discovery of the periodic table, which advanced the atomic theory announced by Dalton in 1812 at a meeting of the Society.

One of the least photographed streets in Manchester is Princess Street, formerly David Street, which links Cross Street with Mosley Street, Portland Street and Whitworth Street. The street originally came into existence in about 1792 when the first houses were erected close to the River Tib, overlooking the site of St Peter's Church. This photograph shows the part of Princess Street opposite the town hall where most of the original properties were domestic in scale, but were eventually replaced by larger, more imposing buildings. Further along, beyond the junction with Portland Street, Princess Street becomes a street of warehouses, many of which were erected in the 1860s and 1870s.

The building at the corner of Cross Street and John Dalton Street was originally a private house, but it was converted into a public house known as the Princes Tavern in about 1828. The importance of this building is not in its architecture, nor events which went on when it was a public house, but in the fact that Thomas de Quincey, author of *Confessions of an English Opium-eater*, was born in the building in 1785. The building was sold at auction for £14,300 in 1885 and demolished in 1889. It was replaced by a red sandstone building which until recently was used by a building society. When the new building was erected a cartouche was included on the Cross Street façade giving details about the birth of de Quincey.

Manchester's Town Hall is often regarded as one of the finest Victorian buildings in the country. It was designed by Alfred Waterhouse and completed in 1877. Although the city council wanted Queen Victoria to officially open the building she declined the invitation and so the honour fell to Alderman Abel Heywood, Mayor of Manchester. The new Town Hall was built fronting on to the newly created Albert Square, the centre-piece of which was the Albert Memorial. When the Town Hall was opened there were three days of celebrations including a grand procession where representatives of the various trades in the city marched in front of the mayor carrying symbols of their trade. If the illustration is examined carefully, it will be seen that the Albert Memorial appears to be partly surrounded by scaffolding and that there are barriers in front of the Town Hall. The photograph was probably taken early in 1894, when the Albert Memorial was restored in readiness for Queen Victoria's visit in May of that year to open the Manchester Ship Canal.

Albert Square was created in the mid-1860s when a number of small workshops and back-to-back houses were demolished to create a square in which Manchester's tribute to Prince Albert could be located. The Albert Memorial, handed over to the city in 1867, was designed by Thomas Worthington to house a statue of the Prince that had been given to Manchester by Alderman Goadsby. Within a short space of time several other statues were added. The first was of James Fraser, Bishop of Manchester, which was unveiled in 1888. The next one, unveiled in 1891, was of John Bright, who was one of the leaders of the Anti-Corn Law League and Free Trade in Manchester. Bright's statue can be seen in this photograph of Albert Square between the wars, just to the left of the Albert Memorial. The final statue to be added was of William Gladstone, unveiled in 1901, and on the left of the picture. The original paved area in Albert Square was very much smaller than it is today, as this photograph shows. Since 1945 the roadway has been reduced so that by the time of writing Albert Square has been almost completely pedestrianized.

Peter Street was created in 1793 to link Oxford Street, which was then under construction, with Deansgate and Quay Street. As a result vehicles wanting to get to the Castlefield and the Bridgewater Canal or Mersey Irwell Navigation did not have to work their way down Market Street, but could take the new road. This saved time and reduced congestion in central Manchester – the aim of building the road was to try to reduce congestion on Market Street. To many people Peter Street is associated with Peterloo, the Free Trade Hall, Theatre Royal, the Midland Hotel and the Gaiety Theatre. This view shows the side of Peter Street facing the Free Trade Hall and Theatre Royal. The building on the right is the Comedy Theatre, later renamed the Gaiety Theatre. The Comedy Theatre was built in 1884 as a replacement for the Gaiety Theatre of Varieties which was destroyed by fire in the previous year. As a theatre it had a reputation for having poor sight lines for the audience in certain parts of the building, a problem which was never properly resolved. In 1903, after a change of ownership, it was renamed the Gaiety Theatre, although it did not result in a change of the type of play put on. In 1908 Annie Horniman began the first permanent repertory theatre in the country. Horniman put on plays that were chosen for their quality. Likewise, the actors and actresses were engaged because of the quality of their performance. Among the plays that were first performed at the Gaiety under Horniman were *Hindle Wakes* and *The Whispering Well*. The Gaiety Theatre closed as a theatre in 1921 and was converted into a cinema, which was demolished in 1959.

One of Manchester's best known and probably best loved buildings is the Free Trade Hall on Peter Street. This building, designed by Edward Walters, was completed and opened in 1856, replacing two earlier temporary buildings which had been erected on the site by the Anti-Corn Law League to hold fund raising events in the 1840s. The building shown in this illustration was used not only for public meetings, but also for exhibitions, political meetings and concerts. It was the first public hall in Manchester which could be used for events irrespective of political and religious persuasions. It was also the only public building in the country which was named not after a local person or a saint, but after an economic idea, free trade. The Free Trade Hall became the home for the most famous series of concerts held in Manchester by the Hallé Orchestra. These were started in 1858 and ran continuously since then, with the exception of the Second World War, until 1996, when the orchestra moved to its new home, the Bridgewater Hall on Lower Mosley Street. Among the meetings which have taken place in the building have been suffragette meetings, meetings in support of the Manchester Ship Canal and meetings addressed by political leaders such as Churchill in January 1940. As well as events of public interest, the Free Trade Hall was also a popular venue for school speech days and on occasions celebratory dinners. It is interesting to note the canopy over the pavement which allowed those attending events to descend from their carriages or cabs and enter the building without getting wet.

As Manchester expanded outwards at the end of the eighteenth century, new roads came into existence while existing roads changed from country lanes to busy streets. An example of the latter was Liverpool Road, which until 1806 was known as Priestnor Street. One reason given for the change of name was that now Eccles New Road was open, the road between Manchester and Liverpool had been improved and this was the quickest way to reach the new turnpike road. The earliest houses on Liverpool Road were constructed in the 1790s and are shown in this photograph. In the mid-nineteenth century these houses were in multi-occupation with families living in the cellars. At street level shops predominated, selling a wide range of goods. In 1891, about five years before this photograph was taken, the shops included a clothier, ladder maker, several furniture brokers, a butcher, several beer retailers, a boot maker and a tobacconist. Although the photograph does not identify where on Liverpool Road the photograph was taken, it is possible to make an assumption that it shows the part of Liverpool Road between Southern Street and Barton Street, where in 1891 the shops were occupied by a furniture broker, a fent dealer, a ladder maker, a butcher and a hairdresser. Ten years later the fent dealer and the furniture broker had moved on, replaced by a fishmonger and a tripe dealer.

The Three Sugar Loaves public house stood at the corner of Water Street and Back Quay, across the road from the River Irwell. It is not certain when it opened, but it was certainly in existence in 1772 when the first Manchester directory was published. It is possible that it was built in the 1750s or 1760s to provide for the men who were working at the various wharves which had been established on the banks of the River Irwell by the Mersey Irwell Navigation. For a time in the 1820s it was known as the Navigation, but reverted to its original name before 1845. The building shown here must have been a rebuild of the earlier one, but it is not recorded when this took place; neither is it known when it closed and was demolished. This might have been during the Second World War or when Manchester redeveloped the area, erecting the College of Building.

The main east-west route through Manchester is along Deansgate, which until the 1870s was a narrow road causing much congestion. The council tried to secure its widening on several occasions, but all attempts failed until they agreed that property owners would be allowed to erect new premises with the same amount of floor space as in their existing buildings. This photograph of Deansgate was taken looking across the road at Barton buildings, whose relatively plain exterior hides one of Manchester's architectural gems, Barton Arcade, designed by Corbett, Raby and Sawyer and completed in 1871. Barton Arcade was one of several shopping arcades which were built in Manchester in the latter half of the nineteenth century, but the blitz and post-war redevelopment has resulted in the loss of all the others. Although the building is much admired today, when it opened some commentators were critical of the height of the shop windows, which, they said, made dressing them effectively very difficult.

When Bury New Road was constructed in the 1820s it ended in a series of narrow streets, which made access to central Manchester very difficult. In order to improve access to and from Bury New Road it was decided to construct a new road from Hunts Bank to Deansgate and St Mary's Gate. This road was known as Victoria Street and its construction divided the Market Place from Smithy Door, which stood adjacent to it and which had been used as an overflow market area in the eighteenth century. In 1876 the area bounded by Victoria Street, St Mary's Gate and Deansgate was cleared, including the remnants of Smithy Door, to enable a new building to be erected, Victoria Buildings, which was destroyed in the blitz. This photograph shows the part of Victoria Street between Victoria Buildings and the Market Place. The building with the gable in the centre is the Coal Exchange while to its right is Sinclair's Oyster Bar, which partially occupies the site of John Shaw's public house of the late eighteenth century. The tower in the background is the ventilation tower of Strangeways Prison, opened in 1868 as a replacement for the New Bailey Prison in Salford.

There has been a church on the site of Manchester Cathedral since before the Norman Conquest. In the middle ages Manchester was the centre of an extensive parish covering 60 square miles of south-east Lancashire, and like many other parishes experienced absentee clergy. In 1422 the Lord of the Manor, Thomas de la Warre, who was also a priest, secured a charter for the church which changed its status from that of a simple parish church to a collegiate church. This allowed for a number of clergy to be appointed with specific instructions to visit the outlying townships as well as conduct services in the parish church. When the church became a college its dedication was also changed to St Mary, St Denys and St George. From 1422, when the charter was granted, until 1847, when the Diocese of Manchester was created, the charter was suspended on several occasions, but the basic principle of several clergymen serving the area was maintained. One result of the collegiation of the parish church was that an extensive programme of rebuilding was undertaken in the fifteenth and early sixteenth centuries which transformed the building. Further work was undertaken in the early nineteenth century and extensive rebuilding had to be carried out in the 1870s to overcome the problems of damage to the stone work caused by pollution. After the rebuilding work of the middle ages only one major addition to the structure of the church was undertaken before the repair of damage caused by the blitz. This was the construction of a porch at the west end to commemorate Queen Victoria's diamond jubilee in 1897. This view of the Cathedral from the early twentieth century shows not only the church but also the site where Hanging Bridge is now displayed and the domes of the Corn Exchange, built between 1892 and 1903.

Linking Victoria Bridge with Corporation Street and Cannon Street is Cateaton Street, which comes from the Anglo-Saxon meaning 'hollow way', behind which runs Hanging Ditch. This view of Cateaton Street shows its junction with Victoria Street in about 1900. The small ornate building in the centre of the illustration is Minshull House, built on land given to Manchester by Thomas Minshull, an apothecary in the seventeenth century, to provide help for the poor and train them in useful occupations. The building shown here was erected in 1889 to the designs of Ball and Elce and is in the Queen Anne style. In the sub-basement of the building are one and a half arches of the medieval Hanging Bridge, which provided access to the churchyard. The building on the left was rebuilt in 1906, about the same time as the remaining arch of Hanging Bridge was exposed as a feature for visitors and Mancunians to see.

Compared with some towns, Manchester's Market Place is relatively small and by the eighteenth century was inadequate for the size of the town and its population. In addition, it attracted people into Manchester from the surrounding area. As well as market stalls, the Market Place also had the town's stocks and pillory as well as a market cross. In 1729 the space was further restricted by the construction of a building called the Exchange, which was intended to encourage merchants to meet together in one place rather than in different parts of the town. It was not a success and eventually, in 1792, the building was demolished. By the nineteenth century most of the buildings in and around the Market Place dated from the eighteenth centuries although one building, the Wellington Inn, was probably built in the sixteenth century. On this photograph, looking towards the Royal Exchange, the Wellington Inn can be identified by the name Will Chambers seen between the first and second floors of the timber-framed building in the centre of the photograph. The building on the right is the Coal Exchange, which was built in the 1860s on the site of the former Victoria Fish and Game Market, demolished in 1865. When most of the market stalls were moved to Smithfield Market in the 1820s a few were allowed to remain, but in 1891 these too were cleared away, as the presence of stalls and people combined with traffic created a dangerous situation on market days. Some stalls, however, were allowed to remain in the area between the Wellington Inn and the Coal Exchange.

One of Manchester's oldest streets is Long Millgate, which is said to be so named because it led to one of the mills on the River Irk, owned by the Lord of the Manor, where townsmen were meant to have their grain ground. Long Millgate ran at the side of Manchester's manor house, which in 1422 was given to the collegiate church to be a home for the clergy. In 1650, the building was acquired by the executors of Humphrey Chetham, who established a school for forty buys of 'poor, painful parents that neither rogues or vagabonds be'. Backing on to Chetham's was Manchester Grammar School, founded in 1515 by Hugh Oldham, Bishop of Exeter. Long Millgate was not a straight road, there being several rather narrow sections and sharp bends. This photograph shows the junction of Long Millgate and Todd Street, close to a spot which was known as Dangerous Corner until 1829 when the road was widened. The building on the right, designed by Richard Lane and opened about 1837, was originally used for the collegiate church's Sunday school. In the background can also be seen the Manchester Arms public house, which was formerly the town house of the Howarth family. It was from the garden of this house that James Saddler undertook the first balloon ascent in Manchester in 1785. The building was demolished in the 1970s as it was in the way of the proposed underground planned for Manchester. The buildings on the left were warehouses and the Old Swan Hotel, both erected in the mid-nineteenth century when Victoria station was expanding.

Until the mid-nineteenth century the Market Place was surrounded by many small courts and passages. The construction of the first part of Corporation Street in 1846 resulted in the clearance of some of these, but many still remained. One such passage was known as Bull's Head Court, which is shown here in the 1930s. The court was originally the entrance to the stable yard of the Bull's Head Hotel which fronted on to the market-place. In the mid-nineteenth century it sold its frontage and turned a side entrance into its main entrance. The large bull's head which was over the original main entrance was moved to a new location over the new main entrance, and a sign was erected across the passage to make sure everyone knew where the hotel was. The bull's head was said to have been part of the crest of the Derby family of Knowsley Hall. Also visible in the background is a large pair of spectacles, often used to advertise opticians.

The construction of Corporation Street was started in the 1840s to improve the route between central Manchester and Cheetham Hill Road and reduce the amount of traffic having to pass through the Market Place, along Old Millgate and Long Millgate to reach York Street (now Cheetham Hill Road). The work was done in two phases, Market Street to Withy Grove and the Withy Grove to Ducie Bridge in the 1850s. One result of the construction of this new road was that an alternative access to Victoria station could be constructed, although it was not until the 1870s that the present roadway in front of the station was completed. The new road enabled buildings to be erected to take advantage of their proximity to the station, although the buildings that originally faced on to Long Millgate were not turned round but continued to face Long Millgate. This illustration shows Corporation Street from near its junction with Miller Street, looking towards central Manchester. On the right can be seen the canopy over the fish dock at Victoria station, which was added in the early twentieth century to handle fish trains from the coast. In the centre of the block of buildings in the middle of the picture is the Manchester Arms public house, which was one of those that continued to have its main entrance on Long Millgate. Today all these buildings have disappeared and the site is a car park.

This photograph of about 1902 shows the junction of Corporation Street and Market Street. At this time the corner building was occupied by Westmacotts, one of Manchester's leading chemists. Next door was a fried fish dealer while Major Drapkin occupied No. 3 Corporation Street. The upper floors of these buildings were offices for a large number of firms. For instance, the firms above No. 9, Victoria Chambers, included a solicitor, heraldic engraver, a disinfectant manufacturer, a watch-maker and a working jeweller. The buildings on the left occupy the site where Marks and Spencers Manchester store was until June 1996.

Until 1829 access to Cross Street from Market Street was through a narrow alley at the side of a public house. With the opening of the town hall on the corner of Cross Street and King Street in 1825 the police commissioners, who formed part of the local government of the town (*see* p. 44), decided that it would enhance the town if the entrance to Cross Street were improved. The result was that the improvements were made at the same time as the alterations to Market Street were being undertaken. Another change which took place at the same time was that the whole length of Cross Street was given a single name, whereas previously there had been three or four different names to the road. Further changes took place in 1866 when the Royal Exchange was rebuilt with a façade on Cross Street, while in 1868 the *Manchester Guardian* established its offices on Cross Street, opposite the Royal Exchange.

CROSS STREET, MANCHESTER.

During the nineteenth and early twentieth century many of the original buildings which lined Cross Street were replaced by stone faced buildings which had shops at street level and offices on the upper floors. This view was taken looking along Cross Street towards the Royal Exchange. Among the buildings it shows is Lloyds Bank (centre), which was erected on the site of the former Manchester Town Hall. One important nineteenth-century resident on Cross Street was J.B. Dancer, who was a scientific instrument maker, undertaking work for scientists like Dalton and Joule. Another well-known resident was Ernest Jones, the Chartist leader, who was a barrister: he had an office in a building that once stood on the site of the building seen here advertising a summer sale.

After the cathedral the oldest church in central Manchester is Cross Street Chapel. This chapel was established in 1694 by the followers of the Revd Henry Newcombe, who had been expelled from the Collegiate Church in 1662 for refusing to accept the Restoration religious settlement. When Cross Street Chapel was established it followed the tenets of Presbyterianism, but during the eighteenth century it gradually moved away Trinitarianism to Unitarianism. The building shown here had been rebuilt in 1715 after it had been severely damaged by rioters supporting the old Pretender. The cost of repairing building was £1,500, which was met by Parliament. In 1929 Cross Street Chapel was described as the 'best brick built building in Manchester', but unfortunately it was destroyed in the Christmas blitz of 1940. A new chapel was erected on the site after the war, but now this has been demolished and a new development occupies the site.

King Street came into existence in about 1735 and was for many years a residential street. It is said that the name was given to it by supporters of the exiled Stuarts who also named a nearby square as St James's Square. For almost a century the only access to King Street was from Cross Street, but in 1829 the King's Arms Coaching House on Deansgate was demolished and an alternative entrance to the street was created. Cross Street divides King Street into two sections, each with a different character. This photograph shows the upper part of King Street looking down from Spring Gardens to Cross Street in the 1860s or '70s. This part of King Street became associated with banking and insurance in the nineteenth century and the presence of such offices was encouraged by the Bank of England, which opened in Manchester in 1825. In the photograph the classical-style building is Cockerell's Bank of England completed in 1845. Beyond the bank can be seen Town Hall Chambers which was later to be replaced by Alfred Waterhouse's offices for the Prudential Insurance Company. In the background are the buildings which were demolished when the Eagle Insurance Company built its offices on Cross Street in 1911. On the right can be seen the edge of the buildings which were also designed by Alfred Waterhouse in 1862 for the Royal Insurance Company, but which were later to be owned by the Vulcan Insurance Company.

The lower part of King Street, between Cross Street and Deansgate, developed in the nineteenth century as a shopping street with many of the houses which had been erected in the eighteenth century being replaced by shops. These new shops tended to cover the whole of the plot of land so that many are long and narrow. The street itself was much narrower than the upper part of King Street and so traffic congestion was always a problem. When this photograph was taken in 1931 parking restrictions had been introduced with the notice informing motorists which side they could park on, the date being the determining factor. Architecturally this part of King Street presents a variety of styles from the mock half-timbering of Nos 15–17 and Old Exchange Passage to the Georgian style of No. 35, the Victorian form of No. 62 and the terracotta character of Liberty's shop, dated 1906. The answer to parking and traffic congestion on this narrow street was adopted in the 1970s – cars were banned and the area pedestrianized.

In 1822 the Police Commissioners, who governed Manchester in conjunction with the manorial Court Leet, decided to replace their offices on Police Street with a purpose-built town hall. Francis Goodwin was commissioned to design the building, which was erected at the corner of Cross Street and King Street on the site of Dr Charles White's house. The new building not only included offices for the Commissioners and their officials, but also for the watch. In 1840, after two years of wrangling, the Police Commissioners handed the building over to the new borough council, who continued to use it until 1877 when the Town Hall in Albert Square was opened. The old Town Hall was then converted into Manchester's Free Reference Library, as the former library building in Castlefield had been declared structurally dangerous and condemned. The library remained in the former Town Hall until 1912 when this building was declared unsafe and the library was forced to move to temporary premises. The old Town Hall was demolished with the columns from the front being re-erected in Heaton Park. This photograph shows the former Town Hall when it was the library. The tower on the right is part of the York Hotel, which was built on the site of the house where the author Harrison Ainsworth was born.

Although many of the buildings on King Street were rebuilt in the nineteenth century, one of the original gentleman's residences has remained, No. 35. This house, which was built in about 1735 by Dr Peter Waring who was an ardent supporter of the Jacobite cause, would have had views across open countryside when completed. In about 1788 the property passed into the hands of the Jones family. When John Jones died, his sons abandoned the tea dealing and concentrated on banking. When Lewis Lloyd married into the family, the bank changed its name to Jones, Lloyd & Co. In 1863 the bank was taken over by the Manchester and District Banking Co., which is now part of the National Westminster Group who continued to use the building as a bank until the 1990s. The railings in front of the property were there to prevent people falling down and injuring themselves as street lighting was non-existent until the nineteenth century. Those who did not rail their cellars were liable to a fine imposed by the authorities.

St Ann's Square, originally known as Acres Fields, was the site of the annual fair held in Manchester from 1222 to 1820, until it was moved first to Smithfield and then to Liverpool Road. In 1708 the size of Acres Field was reduced by the Act of Parliament authorizing the construction of St Ann's Church and a surrounding churchyard 'three score yards in length and forty yards in breadth'. At the same time the right to continue to hold a fair in the area was guaranteed. Originally St Ann's Square was a tree-lined residential area, but towards the end of the eighteenth century the first shops appeared and gradually the domestic dwellings were replaced by shops and offices. This particular view shows St Ann's Square in about 1910 at its junction with Exchange Street. At that time the shops which were on the side shown in this photograph included a silk mercer, a tea dealer, chemist, boot maker, goldsmith and hairdresser while on the opposite side there was a tailor, a cook and confectioner's shop, bookseller, ladies outfitter and a photographer. In the offices above the shops there were a wide range of small businesses, most of a professional or consultancy nature. Today many of the buildings on this side of the square retain the same character and appearance as they did over a century ago. The photograph also shows the buildings on the Deansgate side of Exchange Street, facing the Royal Exchange, which have all been replaced by modern buildings.

In 1775 an Act of Parliament was promoted which allowed certain improvements to be made to Manchester, including the opening up of a road from St Mary's Gate into St Ann's Square. This road became known as Exchange Street and provided an improved access to the square as well as opening up a view of St Ann's Church. To create Exchange Street it was necessary to demolish a number of buildings both on St Mary's Gate and in the square itself. This pre-First World War view shows the ground floor level of the Royal Exchange before it was extended in 1919. The statue in the centre of the picture is dedicated to those who fought in the Boer War and was unveiled in 1908. The number of hackney carriages in the photograph are a reminder that it was from St Ann's Square that distances to and from Manchester were measured and that the square was also an official hackney carriage stand.

Market Street, originally known as Market Stede Lane, developed in a piecemeal manner as the town extended outwards over the centuries. By the eighteenth century it linked the Market Place with Levers Row and the Daub Holes (Piccadilly), but its width was irregular and it was a fairly steep road. Although improvements were made to some streets in the late eighteenth century, Manchester Street was not regarded as a priority case. It was not until 1821 that permission was obtained to undertake a major widening of the road, a project which cost over £250,000 and took well over a decade to almost complete, the final section not being undertaken until the 1870s. This photograph was taken in about 1910 and shows the corner of Corporation Street and Market Street, looking towards Piccadilly, with buildings which were demolished when the Arndale Centre was built. The shop on the corner was that of the firm of J.S. Moss, gentlemen's outfitters and tailors founded in about 1792 and described as a cash rather than credit tailor with a high class clientele. The S stands for Slazenger. It was the son of the founder who went to London and founded the well-known sports wear firm in the nineteenth century.

The final stage of the improvement of Market Street took place when Palace House was demolished in about 1870. This building got its name in 1745 as it was the home of Mr Dickenson who accommodated Bonnie Prince Charlie when he passed through the town in December 1745. This view of Market Street, looking towards Piccadilly, was taken in 1937 when the street was decorated for George VI's coronation. The lack of traffic is unusual as normally Market Street was one of the most congested streets in central Manchester which, even before the arrival of the internal combustion engine, some commentators regarded as dangerous to cross. Although it was pedestrianized in the 1980s, the original idea to remove traffic from this important road was first made by the city engineer in 1906.

Market Street in the 1960s, showing some of the buildings on the left hand side (looking towards the Royal Exchange) which were demolished to make way for the Arndale Centre. Although part of this side of Market Street around the junction with Cross Street has been demolished, there are still a number of buildings on this side which date back to the nineteenth century and show the style of building which graced both sides of Market Street until relatively recently.

Another view of Market Street in the 1960s, but this time the opposite side of the road. All these buildings were demolished to make way for the Arndale Centre. The area behind these buildings consisted of warehouses and small dark courts, many of which bore the names of those who had either owned property there or lived there. To go behind the shops on Market Street even in the 1950s and 1960s was to enter another world.

One corner that has changed dramatically in the last ninety years is that where Market Street and Mosley Street meet Piccadilly. This picture shows the corner in about 1905 when the site was occupied by the Royal Hotel. This hotel had moved here in 1827 when its original site on High Street was required for a warehouse. The building itself had been erected in about 1772 for the Potter family, who sold it in 1814 although continuing to live there until it was purchased by Henry Lacy. When the Royal Hotel opened it leased some of the property at the rear to David Bannerman for use as a warehouse, which gave rise to the comment that within twenty years Moseley Street would cease to be a residential street and become one of shops, offices and warehouses. The Royal Hotel was demolished in 1908 and replaced by Royal Buildings. In the background is the tower which was a feature of Lewis's store in the early twentieth century. It was the arrival of Lewis's which revolutionized shopping in Manchester by opening on Saturdays and catering for the rising middle and lower middle classes. Their bold approach caused friction with the more traditional shops like Finnigans and Kendals, who sought to offer a personalized service and were fearful of their new competitor.

There are a number of springs under central Manchester. Several of these were used in the sixteenth century to supply water for the conduit in the Market Place. Their existence is probably the reason for the name of Fountain Street, which runs from Market Street towards Cooper Street and Princess Street. Among the buildings on Fountain Street is the former Board of Guardians Office of the Manchester Poor Law Union and the Shakespeare Inn. This inn has a black and white half-timbered appearance, but it is not a creation of the sixteenth century, but the late nineteenth century, when there was a revolt against Gothic architecture. Further along, on the corner of Market Street and Fountain Street, can be seen the buildings which were erected when Market Street was improved.

Oldham Street takes its name not from the fact that it leads to Oldham Road and the town of Oldham, but from Adam Oldham who owned land at the corner of Piccadilly and a lane leading off the square in the late eighteenth century. By the end of the nineteenth century Oldham Street was a favourite shopping street with the ladies of Manchester. It was said that it was possible to buy everything from the cradle to the grave from the shops on Oldham Street. This photograph was taken in the 1890s.

The shops which lined Oldham Street in the nineteenth and early twentieth century became less impressive and important the further away from Piccadilly they were. This photograph shows the corner of Piccadilly and Oldham Street. On the left is Saqui and Lawrence, jewellers who occupied a building erected in about 1881, while on the opposite corner is the Albion Hotel. Other important buildings on Oldham Street in the nineteenth century included Affleck and Brown's store, which was established in 1860 and merged with Pauldens in 1930, and the Oldham Street Methodist Chapel, which was also the headquarters of the Manchester and Salford Methodist Mission.

MANCHESTER *from the Air*

This interesting view of Manchester was taken between the wars and shows central Manchester from the west, looking eastwards towards Piccadilly. At the bottom there is Oxford Road station with its terminal platforms for the electric trains to Altrincham. Also visible is the Refuge Assurance Offices with its distinctive tower, the Palace Theatre and St James Buildings all on Oxford Street. Behind the buildings on Oxford Street there is the Rochdale canal and the Dickenson Street power station, whose chimney is in the centre of the picture. At the top left hand corner of the view is Piccadilly Gardens. Between Piccadilly and Oxford Street are many of the textile warehouses which were important elements in the chain of producing and selling cotton and cotton goods. This view provides a unique opportunity to see this part of central Manchester from an unusual angle.

MARKETS & SHOPS

Surviving medieval documents relating to the manor of Manchester indicate that in the thirteenth century there were those in Manchester who earned their living by buying and selling goods. By 1552 there was a well-established market in Manchester which was subject to certain rules and regulations imposed by the Court Leet, although they might have been suggested by the lord of the manor's steward in order to ensure that trading was carried out in an organized manner. Certain trades, such as the butchers and fishmongers, were allocated specific places within the market-place and when they moved attempts were made to ensure they returned their designated locations. Officials were reported to ensure that trading took place in an open manner, and that certain standards were kept.

As Manchester became more urbanized so the demand for food from the surrounding area increased. Regulations were introduced which were intended to ensure that all those who lived in the township of Manchester were able to purchase sufficient food for their requirements before 'strangers', that is those from the surrounding area. The whole operation of buying and selling was carefully controlled by the lord of the manor as he had a financial interest in all purchases by charging a toll on goods and on shopkeepers.

During the eighteenth century the Market Place became overcrowded and spread into surrounding areas, like Smithy Door. There were also attempts in the 1780s to establish rival markets, such as the one at Newmarket off Cross Street, but these failed as the lord of the manor was prepared to take legal action to protect his interests. However, he did acknowledge that the original market-place was overcrowded and allowed some specialist markets to move into other parts of the town, such as the Apple Market to Fennel Street. Eventually, in the 1820s, it was decided that all the markets should be concentrated at Shudehill.

As Manchester was the centre of the area not only did retail markets develop, but also wholesale markets in foodstuffs as well as in other goods, such as cotton. It is the food markets that attract the most attention as it made the Shudehill area busy throughout the day, and especially in the early hours of the morning.

As well as the markets, shops also developed, many of which specialized in particular types of goods. During the nineteenth century the streets of central Manchester gradually lost their residential character and became streets of shops and warehouses. The first shop, for instance, appeared in St Ann's Square in the 1790s and gradually shops came to predominate in the area. Likewise when Market Street was widened in the 1820s, it was the shopkeepers who were most affected. The retail trade was regarded as very important in Manchester and was able to get its way in certain circumstances. For example, when Deansgate was widened in the 1870s the shops which were affected were able to make a very good deal with the council in return for giving up their existing premises.

Although many of the shops were originally owner-run businesses, gradually some started to establish branches in different parts of central Manchester while others began to develop into what might be called department stores. One of the earliest of these was Kendalls on Deangate, but after 1877 they had a rival in Lewis's on Market Street who appealed to the rising middle class white-collar workers, encouraging them to enter the shop without obligation to purchase anything.

As well as the shops central Manchester has always had a large number of street traders and barrow boys selling a wide range of goods from newspapers to flowers and fruit and vegetables. Although they tend to be spread throughout the city centre, there were certain areas where particular types of street trader could be found, such as those selling second hand books on Shudehill Hill, or the ice-cream sellers around Smithfield market and in Piccadilly.

When the lord of the manor decided to concentrate all the markets on the site at Shudehill, known as Smithfield, it was an open area with little cover except market stalls which the traders erected. The first traders were transferred to Smithfield in 1822, but a small residual market was left in the market-place. In 1845 the borough of Manchester purchased the manorial rights, including those of controlling the markets, from the Mosley family. Gradually the open market was covered over with a cast-iron and glass structure to provide better conditions for the traders. Although there were retail markets at Smithfield, they were better known for their wholesale markets, for fruit, vegetables and fish. This scene was photographed at the end of the nineteenth century, and shows the market hall erected by the council and the large number of people who were to be found in the area when the market was trading.

This scene was photographed in 1896 inside the fruit and vegetable market. Stall holders either await customers or carry on trading as if the photographer were not present, while porters wait for their next job of taking goods which had been brought by greengrocers to the carts to transport back to their shops in central Manchester and the suburbs. At the end of each day's trading goods which were perishable or which were damaged and could not be sold were often passed on to members of the public at very low prices, or just thrown away, to be scavenged by those living in areas like Ancoats or Angel Meadow.

Manchester has always had a number of street traders or barrow boys selling fruit and vegetables. This man selling Kent cherries at 2d a pound in about 1933 was trading in front of a firm called Burma Gems. The cherries look far larger than those which can be purchased today.

These two flower sellers are trading in front of Woolworth's store in Piccadilly.

One of the best known street markets in Manchester was where second hand book sellers concentrated on Shudehill. Book bargains appear to be the object of these browsers and it certainly was a place where bargains could be found. With the development of the Arndale Centre the location for the bookstalls had to be moved. Today only one remains on a pitch at the corner of High Street and Church Street, a pale shadow of the former bustling book stalls of the inter-war years and the 1950s and 1960s.

This street trader is said to be selling 'lucky white heather'. He appears to be on Market Street in front of the Rylands building, across the road from Lewis's store.

A newspaper was published in Manchester in the 1720s, but since 1752, when the *Manchester Mercury* was first published, newspaper publishing has been unbroken in the city for almost 250 years. Some papers only lasted a few years, but others survived for several decades. Many of the newspapers which were published had specific political allegiances such as the *Manchester Guardian* for the Liberals and the *Manchester Courier* for the Tories. Although there were newspaper sellers who worked in the morning, it was often the evening papers which brought them most of their business as people purchased them on the way home to read on the train, tram or bus. This particular newspaper seller appears to have posed for the photographer possibly in Stephenson Square sometime in the 1930s.

This newspaper seller is standing in the Shambles in 1937 with copies of the *Manchester Evening Chronicle*.
The *Chronicle* was one of two evening papers that were on sale in Manchester for over sixty years. It was
first published on 10 May 1897 when 169,000 copies were sold, mostly by boys on street corners. The
first issue was six pages long, but later issues were of eight pages, and even more in the twentieth century.
The paper was founded by Edward Hulton, who also established the *Sporting Chronicle* and the *Athletic News*
as well as the *Sunday Chronicle*, whose political views were inclined towards the Toryism and Tory
democracy as expressed by Disraeli and which appealed to Lancashire working men who supported the
Conservative party at the end of the nineteenth century. Hulton sold his papers in 1924 to Allied
Newspapers, later Kemsley Newspapers. About the same time the paper moved from the premises on
Withy Grove, which it had occupied for almost the whole of its life, to a new building on the corner of
Corporation Street and Withy Grove, which has been known variously as Kempsley House, Thompson
House and Maxwell House. Hulton's papers had a strong interest in sport, which may account for the
newspaper poster the seller is holding.

In the late nineteenth century there were a number of ice-cream makers and sellers in Manchester, many of whom came from Italy. They tended to live close together in the Ancoats area. They made their ice-cream in their own homes, often in the cellars, and from there set out to sell their product to the general public around the streets of Manchester. One of the favourite areas for these Italian ice-cream salesmen was around Smithfield Market, which was always very busy. It is possible that this ice-cream salesman, photographed by Samuel Coulthurst in about 1890, had set up his pitch in the Smithfield Market area.

Another well-known site in Manchester in the late nineteenth century was the hen market on Shudehill. In 1869 it was described as 'a heterogeneous mass of hampers, hen coops and hutches containing poultry, pigeons and rabbits. Most breeds of fowl are represented here . . . '. The commentator went on to report that it was also possible to purchase geese and 'occasionally peacocks, ducks, ferrets and white mice.' The dress of the tradesmen was described as being 'dingy'. This photograph was taken some twenty years later, in about 1890, and shows a boy selling pineapple juice in ½d and 1d glasses.

The Italian ice-cream manufacturers and salesmen gradually improved not only their products but also their stalls. This particular salesman was photographed in the 1930s at the hen market on Shudehill. According to Anthony Rea's book on the Italian community in Manchester, Luigi Rocca, who might be related to the person selling the ice in the picture, was one of the first ice-cream makers in Manchester in about 1881. The Roccas were also involved with Louis Colaluca in manufacturing ice-cream wafers in a factory on Mill Street in Ancoats, this factory being one of the three in the Manchester area between the wars manufacturing ice-cream wafers and cones.

Mrs Spring's shop in Hulme was a general grocery store. It is a reminder of the days when the corner shop sold everything from food to polishes. Clearly visible is the bacon slicer which would have been used to slice bacon to the thickness individual customers required. The left hand advertisement is for a well-known brand of tea, Hornimans, while other products include polish, yeast and something with the name 'laxpur.' Also there are jars and tins on the shelves, but their labels are not clear enough to read.

In the days before photocopying and easy reproduction methods if a business wanted labels or leaflets they would probably have gone to a firm which specialized in ticket writing. These were often small businesses located in small workshops throughout the city. One such firm was that of Frederick Tapp, whose premises were at 56 Thomas Street. Tapp established his business in about 1861 and presumably prospered as this postcard, which may have been used for advertising purposes, was produced in about 1900. The building is still there today, occupied by a firm which is still producing and selling posters for sales, special offers an so on.

There were many small specialist shops in Manchester up to 1939. Although many were located in the suburbs there were still a large number in central Manchester like this pet shop, Princess Aviaries, which described itself as a 'livestock emporium.' The owner certainly sold more than birds because the chalk notices at the side of the door refer to tortoises from 1s each, puppies, monkeys, dogs and young rabbits, while in the cage on the floor are chickens. Some of the cages higher up also appear to have birds in them while in the window an animal appears to be sleeping. The business must have been reasonably profitable as he is on the telephone at a time when such things were far from usual.

Seymour Mead was a well-known and respected grocery chain that was founded in Manchester in about 1865. The company soon acquired a reputation for selling unadulterated tea, coffee and general groceries. Seymour Mead blended their own tea for all their forty branches, a process which took two days. Once all the supplies for their own shops had been completed, Seymour Mead went on to blend tea for other grocers. This window display, photographed in 1908, was prepared for the seventh Grocers' Exhibition held at the St James Hall on Oxford Street, an event which was described as the 'shop window of the grocery trade.' As well as displaying the latest products, shops were encouraged to enter their staff in competitions such as tea matching, window-dressing, bacon slicing and butter and margarine tasting. The photograph also provides a good indication of the packaging in use at the time and prices which were paid for goods.

One of Manchester's best known shops is Kendals on Deansgate. The shop owes its origins to James Watts senior who opened a shop on the corner of Deansgate and Parsonage in 1796. Later he moved to 99 Deansgate on the opposite side of the road. In 1836 the Watts family decided to concentrate on the wholesale side of their business and sold the retail side to three employees, Messrs Kendal, Milne and Faulkner. The shop prospered throughout the nineteenth century and grew in reputation. In 1872 the old building was demolished when Deansgate was widened and a new building erected. Gradually the company extended its premises on both sides of Deansgate. On the north side of Deansgate, the old buildings were demolished and a new one constructed, so that by 1920 permission was given which allowed the two shops on opposite sides of Deansgate to be linked by an underground passage, enabling customers to pass between the two shops without going outside and having to cross the busy Deansgate. This view of part of Kendals is undated, but was probably taken in the 1930s. It shows one of the floors ready to receive its customers at the start of the day.

During the 1890s the buildings between St Mary's Street and Blackfriars Street were cleared to make way for further improvements to Deansgate. When the work took place, evidence was found of medieval buildings dating back to the fifteenth century. Among the businesses which were affected by this redevelopment was that of John A. Phillips, picture dealer, whose shop at No. 84 appears to be attracting a good deal of attention from potential customers. Next door at No. 82 was Worrals, a firm of confectioners who were there from about 1883 until 1897. This shop had been a confectioner for a number of years before Worrals had taken it over. The third shop that can be seen is that of John Owen, toy dealer, who occupied the premises from about 1858 until 1893, when it was acquired by a gentleman by the name of Barr.

Saturday afternoon was always an important shopping time for Mancunians. This photograph taken in the 1950s shows the corner of Piccadilly and Oldham Street as shoppers cross Piccadilly towards the Esplanade. In the background is Saqui and Lawrence, the jewellers, and Woolworth's store, opened in 1926.

ALL IN A DAY'S WORK

Manchester as a large town is a product of the industrial revolution when steam power was adapted to drive machinery and when transport improved to enable raw materials and finished products to be carried in bulk to and from the manufactories. Prior to the eighteenth century Manchester did have industry, although it was small scale and based in the home. Much of it was associated with the woollen industry, but it was the arrival of cotton and the developments in textile machinery which benefited Manchester.

Arkwright's water-frame and Hargreave's spinning-jenny were two of several machines which helped to improve production in the textile industry, but it was Crompton's mule, which to be fully effective required something more than human or water power, that brought about the biggest changes. Crompton's mule and the adoption of steam to drive machines were developed roughly at the same time with the result that one benefited from the other. A number of mule-makers who might be said to have been the origins of the engineering industry in the area established themselves in Manchester. Some of these mule-makers, when they found that some of their orders were left on their hands, began to use them to spin cotton. This is how McConnell and Kennedy started in the cotton spinning industry.

Manchester was never a very large producer of cotton, but it was the centre of the industry with the Exchange and warehouses. It was the place which brought together all those involved in the industry whether as manufacturers of yarn, makers of cotton goods or the manufacturers of machinery, bleaches and dyes. Manchester was the centre of the cotton industry, 'Queen of the cotton cities' as A.B. Reach described the town in 1849.

The emphasis on Manchester being the centre of the textile industry has tended to overshadow the fact that the town and its environs was also an important engineering centre. The products made by engineering firms in Manchester ranged from small parts for machines to railway engines. It was the increasing use of steam power and the faster running of machines that led to the development of machines made of metal where all the parts had to fit accurately. It was not possible, as it had been with wooden machines, to shave little bits off. With metal machines everything had to be made accurately. Gradually the machine tool trade developed with people like Joseph Whitworth taking a leading role. Some of the larger engineering works, such as Beyer Peacock's, were to be found just outside the Manchester boundaries in places like Gorton, where land and rates were cheaper, but which were close enough to Manchester to attract both the skilled and unskilled workers they required. Even in the twentieth century engineering in Manchester has kept pace with the changes that were going on: for instance, the establishment of Avro as aircraft manufacturers, the Belsize car factory and Ferranti (electrical engineering).

As well as engineering, Manchester and the surrounding area has developed a chemical industry, often as a result of demands from the textile industry for colours that would not wash out in water or which were different from those already in use. In many respects the demands of the textile industry encouraged the growth of the chemical industry, with firms such as ICI and Clayton Aniline being established.

Manchester had many small firms making a tremendous range of goods in the nineteenth and twentieth centuries. Only a few are recorded in this section; many more were never fully recorded or, if they were, more by chance than a deliberate policy, such as Plant's hat block manufactury in Ancoats above a stable. Although Reach said that Manchester was the capital of the weavers and spinners it was equally the capital of the engineer, the turner and the lathe operator. All were dependent on each other for their success.

This aerial photograph of Ancoats was taken in the mid-1960s and shows the earliest industrial suburb in Manchester. Running left to right across the photograph is Great Ancoats Street while the linear feature running north to south on the right hand side is the Rochdale Canal. Alongside the road at the side of the Rochdale Canal are the former Sedgewick Mill and McConnell and Kennedy Mill; both were originally engaged in the manufacture of cotton yarn. The earliest of these mills dates from the 1790s, when multi-storeyed buildings were unusual and towered over the surrounding domestic properties. To the south of Great Ancoats Street, also close to the Rochdale Canal, is Brunswick Mill, built in the 1820s, but whose fame rests on the fact that A.V. Roe made some of his earliest aircraft in the basement in about 1910. Other features which can be clearly identified are the tower of St Peter's, Blossom Street, which was consecrated in 1862 and although still standing is in a ruinous condition. In the top left hand corner is Victoria Square, built in about 1892 as a tenement block to replace some of the back-to-back houses and cellar dwellings formerly found in the area. The other obvious building which Mancunians will recognize is the *Daily Express* building on Great Ancoats Street. Today much of the area to the right of the Rochdale Canal has been cleared away, but there are large areas of the remaining part of Ancoats shown on this illustration still extant. Many of the former cotton mills are listed and part of a conservation area, but it is essential to find new uses for the mills before they deteriorate as a result of neglect.

The title of this float is 'Cotton'. What the event is and when it took place is not recorded on the photograph, but the presence of a lifeboat in the background suggests that it may have been part of the annual 'Lifeboat Saturday' held in Manchester from the 1890s onwards. The aim was to raise funds for the Royal National Lifeboat Institution, and involved not only representatives from the RNLI but also other organizations in the city. The parade was held on a Saturday afternoon so that those who had been working in the shops and warehouses in the morning could watch the parade before returning home. This photograph must have been taken after 1903 as the Midland Hotel is in the background.

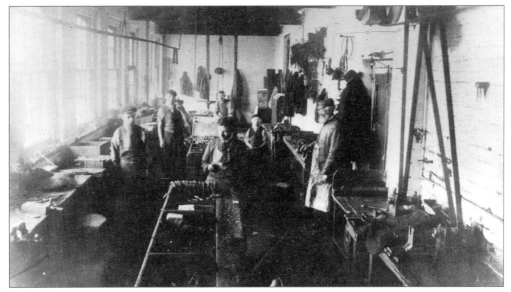

There were many small firms in Manchester in the late nineteenth century. Typical of these was the firm of Pass and Sparey, which was established in about 1880. The firm developed a high reputation for the quality of its spindles which it supplied to the textile trade in Lancashire. The firm was located on Vesta Street, close to the Ashton Canal and a few minutes walk from London Road station so they had two possible ways to send their products to clients. This photograph was taken in about 1900 with William Pass, one of the owners of the firm, keeping a careful eye on his employees and ensuring that as little production time as possible was lost as a result of having a photographer on the premises. Pass and Sparey eventually closed in about 1916 as a result of the First World War.

Although Manchester was an important manufacturing and trading centre in the nineteenth century it was also an important centre for economic ideas, especially that of free trade. In 1837 the Anti-Corn Law League was founded with the aim of securing the repeal of laws which prohibited the import of grain until the price had reached 80s a quarter. Those supporting the movement argued that it kept the price of food artificially high, while those in favour of retaining the corn laws claimed that the reason why the opponents of the corn laws wanted their abolition was so that they could pay lower wages. The organization which developed to run the campaign to secure the repeal of the corn laws was based in Newall's buildings on Market Street, shown in this illustration of 1866 shortly before its demolition to make way for an enlarged Royal Exchange. The Anti-Corn Law League was also responsible for the construction of the early Free Trade Halls in the 1840s, and when they achieved their aim in 1846 they formed a company to build the Free Trade Hall to mark their success and named it after their main economic idea – free trade.

This view shows the Royal Exchange at the corner of Market Street and Cross Street in the early twentieth century. The first Exchange on this site had been opened in 1809, providing a meeting place for businessmen to exchange commercial information and strike deals. In 1851, after Queen Victoria's visit to Manchester and her reception at the Exchange, she granted the title of 'Royal' to the organization. In 1866 it was decided to rebuild the Royal Exchange as it was too small for the growing membership. The new building, designed by Mills and Murgatroyd, was opened in two stages, in 1871 and 1874. By the beginning of the twentieth century its membership had exceeded 10,000 with days of 'High Change' being Tuesdays and Thursdays. The massive portico on the Cross Street façade was demolished in about 1912 to enable Cross Street to be widened.

This is the scene outside the Royal Exchange on Cross Street in about 1910 as businessmen hurry about their business or exchange information and news. It was said that as much business was transacted outside the Exchange as on the floor of the building itself. Across the road from the Royal Exchange can be seen the offices of the *Manchester Guardian*, founded in 1821 as a supporter of the moderate radical movement in Manchester. Later it became associated with liberalism in British politics. The *Manchester Guardian* moved to these offices in about 1868 after it had taken over the *Manchester Evening News*. The *Manchester Guardian* was regarded as the voice of Manchester's free trade movement.

In the nineteenth century Manchester was also an important engineering centre with many companies making a wide range of products which were exported to various parts of the world. One such company was the locomotive manufacturing firm of Beyer Peacock and Co., which was established in Gorton in 1854. The site was chosen because it was outside the borough of Manchester and hence had lower rates, yet close enough to attract the skilled workers it required. The locomotives it built were of all sizes from small tank engines to massive articulated Beyer Garratt locomotives. This photograph shows a small saddle tank built in 1861 for the Knighton Railway, appropriately enough called 'Knighton'. When it was built it cost £1,300, on which the company made a reasonable profit.

It is difficult to associate the chemical industry with the textile industry, but the demands of bleachers and dyers for a wide range of colours, and colours which would not wash out in water, encouraged the development of this industry. This photograph, taken in about 1933, shows the Clayton firm of Clayton Aniline, which had been founded by Charles Dreyfus in 1876 to manufacture dyes from coke oven benzole. Gradually the range of products increased as did the size of the firm, which became part of CIBA in 1911. Note the extensive use of wood in the building, as this would absorb the chemicals, and the clogs the workmen are wearing.

The manufacture of cameras and the taking of photographs required a great deal of precision and care. Manchester developed a reputation for having some very high quality makers of scientific instruments. The most famous was probably J.B. Dancer, who made scientific instruments for scientists like John Dalton and J.P. Joule. He was also something of a photographer, developing the lantern slide and micro-photograph. There were other firms who made scientific instruments for the scientists, hospitals and academic institutions. Among these was the firm shown in this photograph taken in the 1890s, Ronchettl's, later Casartelli's, which was said to be the largest establishment of its type outside London. The firm's involvement in scientific instruments was a sideline as their main business was optical work.

At the end of the nineteenth century the engineering firm of Brooks and Doxey employed about 2,000 men at factories in Miles Platting and Gorton. The firm had been founded by Samuel Brooks in 1859 in Union Mill, Minshull Street in central Manchester to manufacture loom temples and small accessories and tools for the textile industry. Demand for the company's products increased rapidly so that within four years of establishment Brooks was employing over sixty people. As demand grew so did the labour force, with the result that the firm outgrew its original premises and in 1865 moved to Gorton, which is the factory shown here. Presumably the men are leaving work after a hard day in the factory. Twenty-five years later, in 1888, the firm took over the Junction Iron Works in Miles Platting to expand production further.

The period between 1918 and 1939 was one when new industry began to replace the old heavy industries. One of the firms which benefited from this was Ferranti's. Originally Ferranti's was involved in the manufacture of equipment for large generating stations, but Sebastian de Ferranti was also interested in the application of electricity for domestic purposes and for domestic equipment, such as electric irons and fires. As well as manufacturing household products, Ferranti also manufactured radio valves, cathode ray tubes and other specialist electrical devices. In 1934 the company moved into the manufacture of radios, but this was not a great commercial success. This particular illustration shows women assembling radio valves in November 1934 at the company's factory at Moston, which had recently opened.

In an industrialized society one of the problems has been unemployment which has varied according to the state of trade. In 1908 the Manchester area suffered from one of its cyclical periods of high unemployment. Attempts were made to find employment for those out of work, such as landscaping a new park in Rusholme, now known as Platt Fields. Meetings were also held in the town hall to discuss the problem. In 1908 the Dean of Manchester made some comments about the unemployed which were regarded as derogatory – this led to a large crowd gathering outside the Cathedral, shown here. There was also trouble in Albert Square, where a force of 800 police were unable to keep order and arrest the ringleaders. There was a fear on this occasion that the crowd of unemployed might storm the Town Hall and do serious damage to the building.

Industrial relations in industry varied between firms. In the case of the wire-makers Richard Johnson & Nephew in the Bradford district of Manchester, industrial relations were reasonable until the company began to look for economies and brought in a firm of time and motion experts to advise them. One suggestion was to stop the men in the cleaning department working continuous overtime. The men objected to being regarded as machines and walked out on strike. The strike lasted ten months and ended when the firm said that all the posts held by the striking workers had been filled. Here the strikers are seen walking to the factory to collect their tool boxes.

Like all large towns and cities Manchester was affected by the General Strike in 1926. Transport and the distribution of food supplies was severely hit. There were also spasmodic outbreaks of violence with lorries being attacked in areas like Oldham Road. Local newspapers published a small edition. This view shows the crowds outside the *Manchester Evening News* offices in Cross Street shortly after the latest news bulletin had been issued.

When the Borough of Manchester was created in 1838 a watch committee was established, but the Court Leet and the Police Commissioners, who had governed Manchester up to that time, refused to acknowledge the legality of the borough council or any of its committee. It was not until 1842 that Manchester was able to appoint its first Chief Constable, Captain Edward Willis. Over the next century the duties of the police were increased, including point duty at busy junctions such as Cross Street, Corporation Street and Market Street. It was claimed in the early twentieth century that the presence of police on point duty there speeded up the flow of traffic, although some people had other ideas. This photograph, taken in the 1890s, shows a Manchester police officer walking down Market Street, possibly near the Royal Exchange. Whether he is on traffic duty or just patrolling is not clear.

Fire was regarded as a major hazard in towns and villages so precautions were often taken to prevent it either breaking out or spreading. The duty of the night watches which were appointed was to look out for fire rather than law breakers. The earliest recorded fire precautions in Manchester date from 1566, while the earliest record of fire fighting equipment is to be found in the Court Leet records of 1613. Until the arrival of piped water with sufficient pressure there were always difficulties when fighting fires, especially those involving industrial premises where grease and oil added to the problems. Improvements to the fire service were only brought about gradually. In 1899 the watch committee, who were responsible for the fire service in Manchester as well as the police, purchased the horse-drawn fire escape shown in this picture. It was built by William Rose of Salford at a cost of £145. It was the beginning of a series of improvements which culminated in the construction of a new fire service headquarters at the junction of London Road and Whitworth Street and the development of street alarms linked directly to the central fire station, which speeded up response times and reduced the damage fires could cause to buildings.

The York Stone flags which were used for paving the streets of Manchester and other towns provided street artists with an ideal surface on which they could show their artistic talent. This pavement artist is chalking on the flags in Albert Square, in front of the town hall, oblivious to pedestrians going about their normal business. On occasions such pavement artists would attract small crowds to admire their work. Note the bag or cap to the artist's left into which members of the public could throw a coin. This was a hard way to earn a living and in all probability did not earn the artist very much at all.

Remove the tarmac from many of the roads of central Manchester and underneath will be found the original road surface, granite or sandstone setts. These were laid by hand on a sand base held in place by tar being poured into the joints. The difference between setts and cobbles is that cobbles are irregular in shape, while setts are regular, being either rectangular or square. In some places, especially around the infirmary in Piccadilly, where quietness was important, wooden setts were used instead of the more traditional stone ones, which these men are laying at an unidentified location in central Manchester between the wars.

Although many thousands of people used to travel into Manchester by bus and tram there were also a large number of people who travelled by train into central Manchester. In the early years of the twentieth century, it was claimed that 93,000 people used Victoria station every day, although not all these would have been commuters. The people who travelled into Victoria station would have come from east Lancashire, places like Blackburn, Burnley, Nelson and Colne, Bolton, Bury and Rochdale as well as from Liverpool, Southport, Blackpool and Yorkshire. This photograph, dating from the 1940s or 1950s, shows platform thirteen at Victoria station as a train arrives, but there is no indication where from. Between the wars this platform was used by trains from Liverpool and Southport. The type of carriage gives the impression that it might have been a local train as the stock appears to be compartment as opposed to corridor stock, used on trains going longer distances.

Drinking fountains and horse troughs were features which were introduced in the latter half of the nineteenth century. The one shown above appears to have been the gathering point for a group of men. Whether these people were taking a break from their normal work, seeking employment or just watching the world go by is not known, neither is the location of the drinking fountain. However, the photograph does provide the fashion historian with information on the dress of working men at the end of the nineteenth century. Notice that everyone is wearing a hat of some description, often an indication of their status or occupation. At least one of the men is wearing clogs and two have clay pipes, the manufacture of which employed many people in small workshops. Left: In contrast to the men at the drinking fountain these two businessmen caught on camera in the late 1930s stand discussing the day's financial news on the steps of the Royal Exchange.

GETTING ABOUT

Since Roman times Manchester has been an important centre for communications and transport. Passing close to the Roman fort was the main route between the legionary bases at Chester and York from which branch roads lead to other forts and settlements in the area. It was these roads which formed the basis of the road system in the area for almost 1,400 years, until the first turnpike roads were built in the area in the eighteenth century. Although there were several turnpike roads leading to Manchester, they all started or stopped short of the centre of the town, with the result that anyone wanting to travel north to south had to pass through Manchester.

Although Manchester is situated on the River Irwell this was not suitable for transporting goods to and from the coast or other parts of the country. Although small vessels were able to reach Manchester it was not until major improvements undertaken by Thomas Steers were completed in 1735 that vessels of up to 50 tons could reach the edge of Manchester. Within thirty years of the improvements being made to the River Irwell the opening of the first canal, between Worsley and Manchester in 1764, and its extension to Runcorn a decade later, ushered in a new era of transport which was reliable and cheap and allowed the bulk carriage of goods over long distances. Not only did industrialists benefit from the canal, but also farmers as their products could be carried cheaply to the expanding towns of the area, enabling these towns to grow without the fear of food shortages. By 1805 Manchester was the centre of a network of canals linking the town with other parts of the country. The ultimate development in the field of water transport was the construction and opening of the Manchester Ship Canal in 1894, which provided Manchester with a direct link to the sea.

Although canals were ideal for the bulk carriage of goods they were slow and could be affected by adverse weather conditions. In 1825 a new form of transport had been introduced in the north-east to carry freight and now it was decided to apply the steam engine not only to pulling freight trains, but also passenger trains. In 1830 the opening of the Liverpool and Manchester Railway ushered in the railway age, when the time taken to get between towns was dramatically reduced. Within about twenty years the basic railway network around Manchester was completed, linking the city with other industrial areas, the ports as well as smaller towns and villages. Not only was the train used for freight and long distance travel, but it also encouraged the growth of the commuter and the outward expansion of towns. One difficulty travellers encountered on the railways around Manchester was that it was not possible to cross from one side of the city to the other by rail, except by a circuitous route and hence the full potential of north-south traffic was never developed. Several schemes were proposed, but it was not until Metrolink was opened that this difficulty was alleviated.

Bus services in the Manchester area can be traced back to 1824 when John Greenwood introduced a horse bus service from Pendleton to the Exchange. Within a short time others had taken up the idea and a network of horse bus services developed linking Manchester with the surrounding areas. The horse buses, although not cheap to travel on, gave an impetus to the development of residential suburbs such as Victoria Park and Greenheys. Gradually fares did fall, helped by the introduction of cheap workmen's fares after 1877 when the horse tram network was constructed. The introduction of low fares encouraged working people to consider moving from the over-crowded areas of the central and inner suburbs to more pleasant areas with better quality housing. In 1901 the electronic tram began to replace the horse tram, ushering in a mode of transport which survived until 1949, when the last trams were withdrawn. However, as the trams faded away so motor bus services replaced them, being regarded as more flexible in the routes they could take.

Finally in 1929 the granting of a licence for Manchester to operate an airport and the opening of Barton airport in 1930 signalled the arrival of air transport. Barton was replaced by Ringway in 1938 and, although war delayed the growth of air travel, this aspect of travel and transport has mushroomed since the 1960s. Today Manchester Airport is one of the busiest and fastest growing in the country.

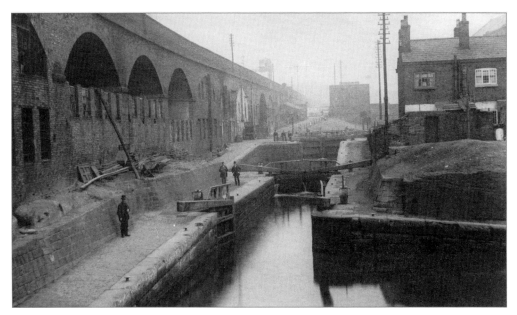

When the Bridgewater Canal was completed there was no direct link between it and the River Irwell. The only way vessels could get on to the river from the canal was to travel to Runcorn and then back along the River Mersey. In 1836 this changed when a clause was included in the Manchester and Salford Junction Canal Act which allowed the Bridgewater Canal to build a lock to provide access to the river. The

Manchester and Salford Junction Canal was 5 furlongs long and was intended to link the Rochdale Canal with the River Irwell at Water Street and reduce the amount of traffic having to be transferred between the two waterway systems by road. The photograph above, taken in about 1892, shows Hulme locks with the lock keepers cottage on the island in the centre. In all, three locks were required to get boats down from the Bridgewater Canal to the River Irwell. The viaduct is that which carries the Manchester to Altrincham railway line. Hulme lock has now been replaced by a new lock providing easier access to the river and Salford Quays. The rather attractive view on the left shows one of Manchester's rivers, the River Medlock, a tributary of the River Irwell, flowing at the back of the Refuge Insurance building in the 1930s. This river was the southern boundary of the township of Manchester. Like all Manchester's rivers and streams it was highly polluted from the various industrial premises on its banks and liable to flooding after heavy rain. The bridge across the river was built in the 1930s to link the Refuge Insurance offices with its car park on the other side of the river.

In 1830 the Liverpool and Manchester Railway was opened, reducing the time it took to get between these two great Lancashire towns from a day to an hour. There were objections to the railway from some of the landowners in the Liverpool Road/Water Street area as well as from the Mersey Irwell Navigation and the Police Commissioners. The Mersey Irwell Navigation insisted that the railway bridge over the river provided sufficient headroom for vessels to continue using the river to reach its warehouses on Water Street. As a result the railway entered Manchester on a viaduct, which included a bridge across Water Street. Water Street bridge, shown here in 1905 just before it was demolished, was manufactured by William Fairbairn in Ancoats, using calculations made by Eaton Hodgkinson to reduce the amount of iron required. The cast-iron sides were added at the insistence of the Police Commissioners in case a train should fall off and damage the road! Note the separation of pedestrians from the road by a line of Doric columns.

When the Liverpool and Manchester Railway commenced its services the only station on the line was at Manchester, and even here it was on the outskirts of the town. This photograph shows that station at the beginning of the twentieth century when it was a goods depot. The house on the left had been built early in the nineteenth century by Mr Rothwell, who had industrial premises in the area, and was already in existence when the station was built and was incorporated into the station. The original station consisted of the rendered section in the centre of the picture. The entrance to the left of the horse and cart was for passengers travelling first class while the second and third class entrances are to be seen behind the horse and cart. On entering the building passengers ascended a staircase to track level, where they boarded the train, there being no platforms in the early days. The remaining part of the building shown in the photograph was constructed in 1831–2 with the intention of providing some shops at street level. However, the shops did not materialize and the whole of this area was appropriated for goods and office accommodation. Liverpool Road station closed as a passenger station in 1844 when services were transferred to Victoria station. It then became a goods depot for the next 130 years until its closure in 1975. Since that time, the buildings have been converted into the Museum of Science and Industry in Manchester.

Victoria station was opened by the Manchester and Leeds Railway (later the Lancashire and Yorkshire Railway) in 1844, replacing its original Manchester terminus on Oldham Road. The new station was also used by the London and North Western Railway, which had taken over the Liverpool and Manchester Railway. Until the mid-1870s the main approach to Victoria station was by way of Hunt's Bank, past the offices of the Lancashire and Yorkshire Railway on the right. The Lancashire and Yorkshire Railway, although one of the smallest in terms of mileage, was one of the major railway companies in the country as it served not only the Lancashire cotton towns but also the industrial towns and coalfields of Yorkshire. During the latter half of the nineteenth century Victoria station was extended several times, and on each occasion the number of platforms was doubled. This view of the approach to the station dates from the 1870s, about the time the number of platforms was being increased from two to four.

The final enlargement of Victoria station took place in the early years of the twentieth century when the number of platforms was increased from eight to seventeen. Not all the platforms allowed trains to run through. Platforms one to ten were terminal platforms for trains from places like Oldham, Rochdale and Bury while platform eleven joined platform four of Exchange station to create the longest platform in Europe. This photograph shows one of the through platforms at Victoria in the 1950s as the class '5MT' locomotive awaits the green flag to depart. Although some passengers appear to be catching this train, others seem to be waiting for another one, possibly a local train to one of the surrounding towns.

Train services to the south of Manchester started and terminated at London Road station (now Piccadilly station). Although owned by the London and North Western Railway, London Road station was shared with the Manchester, Sheffield and Lincolnshire Railway (later the Great Central Railway) in an uneasy relationship. The original station was opened in 1842, but by the 1860s traffic had increased to levels whereby a new station was required. This was completed in 1866 when great care was taken to ensure that the rival railway companies were kept separate and that passengers could easily identify each company's part of the station. The approach to London Road station was up a slope, whose appearance was made even steeper by the fact that London Road dropped away to cross the River Medlock. This view, taken in the years before the First World War, shows that station and its approach from Piccadilly with trams and taxis adding to the transport scene here. The warehouses on the left were built by the Manchester, Sheffield and Lincolnshire Railway and backed on to the terminus of the Ashton Canal, which was owned by the railway.

The arrival of the electric trams in 1901 and the extension of their services to surrounding towns posed a threat to the commuter traffic carried by the railways. In order to combat this competition, the railway companies looked at the possibility of electrifying their lines and speeding up trains. In 1916 the Lancashire and Yorkshire Railway had electrified the line from Manchester to Bury which resulted in an increase in traffic. On the southern side of Manchester, the Manchester South Junction and Altrincham Railway saw their commuter service threatened by trams and responded in 1928 by deciding to electrify the route to Altrincham. Work started in 1929 and was completed by 1931, at a cost of £500,000. The new trains, one of which is shown here, were described as 'big, comfortable and roomy, with a steadiness and smoothness that makes the journey a pleasant break between the offices and the home'. The new electric trains cut five minutes off the journey time between Manchester and Altrincham.

The last of Manchester's mainline stations to be opened was Central station on 1 July 1880. Central station was built by the Cheshire Lines Committee, which was an amalgamation of three companies which did not have their own stations in Manchester, over a section of the Manchester and Salford Junction Canal which had to be closed and filled in. The main feature of the station was the 210 ft span of the arch over the platforms. If the original plan for the station had been adhered to, this arch would not have been visible as there were plans to erect an office block in front of it, but it is said that there were not sufficient funds to do this. This postcard shows the front of the station together with the covered way which was erected when the Midland Hotel was built on a site bounded by Mount Street, Peter Street, Lower Mosley Street and Windmill Street. The aim of the covered way was to ensure guests arriving at the hotel by train did not get wet in the short walk between the hotel and station. Central station closed in May 1969 and after a long uncertain future it was saved and converted into the G-Mex Centre where exhibitions, concerts and events are held. Visitors arriving at G-Mex and parking under the building do so over part of the former canal.

The Cheshire Lines Committee did not have any stock or engines of its own. Those services it ran were done so using equipment leased from its constituent companies. Among the innovations which the Cheshire Lines introduced was a fast, punctual service between Manchester and Liverpool, leaving at half past the hour throughout the day. There were also services to Southport, Chester and through coaches to many parts of the country. The Midland Railway ran services to London St Pancras via the Peak District from Central station, and although the journey time was longer the scenery was very attractive. As well as long distance traffic Central station also had important commuter traffic from the south Manchester area such as Didsbury and Chorlton-cum-Hardy. In many cases it was quicker to travel into Manchester by rail than on the tram, the journey by train only taking ten minutes or so. This atmospheric photograph was taken in 1930 and shows a train arriving while a tank engine, possibly from the London and North Eastern Railway, awaits the all clear to depart with one of the 400 trains which used the station each day.

In 1824 the first horse buses were introduced between Manchester and Pendleton in Salford. The cost of travelling on these early horse buses was expensive, a single journey costing 6*d*. As a result they tended to be used by businessmen travelling to and from their business premises. The early horse bus drivers were kept busy – not only had they to manage the horse, but also to blow a horn to announce the progress of the journey, account for the fares at the end of the journey and help passengers on and off buses. In 1851 larger vehicles were introduced which required three horses and as a result the driver was given an assistant, the guard or conductor, who collected the fares. This horse bus was photographed as it entered Mosley Street from Piccadilly. Although all the passengers on this bus are facing the front, in the early buses those on the upper deck sat facing outwards with their feet resting on a board, so that passengers on the lower deck saw an array of boots and shoes of all shapes and sizes and in various states of repair and cleanness. The smell in the interior of these horse buses were said to resemble that of a stable, especially in wet weather when straw was strewn on the floor.

In 1877 a change took place when horse-drawn trams were introduced. The horse-drawn trams could carry up to forty-two passengers at 7 mph. The tracks were laid by Manchester City Council and rented to the tramway operators at a rate of ten per cent of the cost of construction per annum. The horse trams were more efficient when it came to the use of horse power, but still required a large number of horses to be kept in reserve to ensure that they were changed regularly and not tired out. This photograph shows one of the horse trams operated by the Manchester Tramways and Carriage Company in Manchester. By the time horse-drawn trams were introduced, fares had fallen considerably from the 6d per journey of 1824 and fell even further when the cheap workmen's fares were introduced. There was also a distinction in fares depending on where you sat, with higher fares being charged for those who travelled inside the tramcar.

When the original tram tracks were laid the leases to the operating companies were for twenty-one years. In 1898, when the first leases were due for renewal, the city council had to decide whether to replace the track and electrify the system, and whether it should continue to be operated by private companies or run by the local authority itself. In the end it was decided that the local authority would take over the operation of the system so that profits would be used to subside new routes. The laying of the new tram track appears to have attracted a great deal of attention if this photograph of the junction of Deansgate and St Mary's Gate is any guide. It also appears to have caused a major disruption of traffic circulation in the town with roads having to be dug up.

This photograph of 1902 shows electric trams at the junction of Cross Street, Corporation Street and Market Street. By the end of 1902 about twenty-six electric tram routes were in operation serving, among other places, Cheetham Hill, Blackley, Queen's Park, Gorton, Belle Vue, Middleton, Stockport and West Didsbury. The new electric trams still had open tops, but in about 1905 the first covered cars were introduced. Also visible in the picture is a horse tram; they still operated on some routes for a further two years. The new electric trams provided competition for the railways, especially on services to Bury, where a significant number of passengers were lost to the new form of road transport.

As the electric tramways developed so the tramcars were improved, and the old system of having no roof and open ends on the upper deck gave way to fully enclosed cars as shown in this picture. The tram in the photograph is on the No. 32 route from Victoria Street to Reddish via Market Street, which was converted to bus operation in 1946. This photograph of the 1930s also shows one of the problems which trams created as the amount of road traffic, especially private cars, increased. Trams had to run on fixed tracks so that cars and other road vehicles were forced to one side, and if the street was busy with pedestrians it could be dangerous for those walking at the edge of the pavement.

In 1931 Manchester created a bus station in the city centre, Parker Street bus station, which enabled buses to be kept off the road when waiting for their time to depart. This view shows Parker Street bus station in the 1930s with bus stands, although covered, still open at the sides to the weather.

Before the First World War Manchester suffered from chronic traffic congestion, but the war delayed the implementation of improvement schemes. During the 1920s attempts were made to reduce the congestion with the introduction of one-way systems and parking restrictions. This photograph shows the junction of Portland Street and Oxford Street in 1933 when Portland Street was made one-way. Tram No. 315 in the photograph was introduced in 1929/30 and was photographed here on the no. 41 route from Victoria Street to West Didsbury. Also in the picture are an Austin 7 car and two Crossley bodied buses: the right hand one is bound for Sale Moor while the left hand one is numbered 28 although it is not possible to identify which route it is on. Further attempts were made to reduce congestion five years later in 1938, when a bold scheme was introduced involving a one-way system from All Saints into Manchester and along Princess Street out of the city centre. The full scheme only lasted six months owing to complaints from shopkeepers that it resulted in a loss of business.

The Manchester blitz of Christmas 1940 changed the face of Piccadilly. All the warehouses facing Parker Street bus station were destroyed. After the war, the vacant sites were converted into temporary car parks as the number of private cars coming into the city centre increased. The post-war development enabled the bus station, which had been badly damaged in the blitz, to be planned and upgraded. This 1957 photograph shows work beginning to be done on the new Parker Street bus station together with the car parks where Piccadilly Plaze now stands.

Until the arrival of the internal combustion engine goods were taken to and from factories and warehouses by horse-drawn waggons and lurries. Reach, writing in 1849, commented about the waggons 'high piled with goods, hauling loads which horses must shudder to contemplate'. Even between the wars horse-drawn carts were still in regular usage around the streets of Manchester as this photograph shows.

Waggons and lurries were slow, but suitable for carrying bulk goods. However, there were occasions when a faster form of road transport was required, such as for the delivery of newspapers to newsagents and news vendors in the city centre. This photograph, taken in the 1930s, shows a typical two-wheeled cart used to take small loads quickly around town. It is possible that this cart was delivering the *Manchester Evening News* as it appears to be carrying bundles of newspaper in front of the driver.

The scene as goods vehicles negotiate their way along Portland Street in the inter-war years. Not only are there horse-drawn vehicles and a few private cars, but also a steam lorry, a form of road traction which never really caught on. The buildings which lined Portland Street at this time were mainly textile warehouses. The one on the right was built in the 1860s to the designs of P. Nunn and occupied by the Behrens family.

These police officers appear to be checking the documents of this motorist in a central Manchester street between the wars.

During the inter-war years traffic, particularly that powered by the internal combustion engine, rapidly increased giving rise to congestion in city centre streets. This photograph shows the scene in St Peter's Square as traffic makes its way from Peter Street towards Mosley Street and Piccadilly. Horse-drawn vehicles, cars, lorries and even buses are all mixed up, although it does appear that the horse-drawn cart and the bus are segregated from the motor traffic.

Although aircraft had been in existence since the early years of the twentieth century and planes were being built by A.V. Roe in Manchester in 1910, it was the use of aircraft in the First World War which resulted in developments in aircraft design which ultimately led to the development of passenger-carrying aircraft and the race by local authorities to build airports. On 22 April 1929 Manchester was granted the first licence to operate a municipal airport. The earliest Manchester airport was Rackhouse in Wythenshaw. In 1930 Barton airport opened and services were transferred to the new site, but by 1938 the difficulties of expanding on the site had become apparent and a new site was chosen for Manchester Airport, at Ringway on the edge of Wythenshawe, where there was room for expansion. This photograph shows the Lord Mayor, Alderman George Westcott, and a deputation from Manchester in London to receive the licence for the Manchester airport in 1929. The plane in the background was operated by Northern Air Services (Manchester) Ltd, who claimed to have a fleet of 'modern aircraft'.

In 1938 Manchester moved its municipal airport from Barton to Ringway following criticism of Barton by Captain Smirnoff of KLM. The site for the new airport had been acquired in 1935 at a cost of £53,000 and covered over 600 acres. When the airport was opened in 1938 by Sir Kingsley Wood, Secretary of State for Air, the total investment in the project had already amounted to £175,000. The original plan was to construct the terminal buildings once the airport was open, but with increased traffic and the possibility of international flights it was decided to complete the development of the site as soon as possible. The first international airline to start regular flights was KLM, one of whose planes is shown in this 1938 photograph of Manchester Airport.

A BREAK IN THE
DAILY GRIND

In 1857 Charles Beyer complained that the royal visit to Manchester had resulted in a considerable loss of production and pleaded with Henry Robertson, one of the partners, to come to Manchester to help stir things up. Not only did industry close down for royal visits so did the schools and, as in industry, single days off often extended into two or three more days. During the century after Queen Victoria's first visit to Manchester in 1851 the reigning monarch visited Manchester on several occasions. In all Queen Victoria made three visits to Manchester, Edward VII made two visits, four visits were made by George V and at least two by George VI. By the mid-twentieth century, although royal visits attracted large crowds, they tended not to be the major event they were a century earlier.

As well as royal visits there were local events which were significant. For example, events associated with the opening of Manchester Town Hall in 1877, the Royal Jubilee Exhibition of 1887, not in Manchester but staged very close to its boundaries in Old Trafford, the opening of the Manchester ship canal, which although involving a royal visit in May 1894 had been 'unofficially' open on 1 January 1894, events surrounding Civic Week in 1926 and the centenary of the borough in 1938. Neither should special events which took place in individual communities be overlooked, such as the opening of a new school, town hall or library as these also attracted crowds, just as in the years following the First World War the unveiling of local war memorials were attended by many people from the community.

As well as one-off events, the calendar was also full of events which took place annually and which attracted large crowds of onlookers. Events such at the Shrove Tuesday antics of the students at Manchester University from the late nineteenth century onwards, Whit Walks, Lifeboat Saturday and a host of local events such as the Didsbury Show, started in 1901. Events like these were part of life for people in the nineteenth and early twentieth centuries.

Until the arrival of radio and television the only other means of learning what happened at an event or seeing a personality was to be part of the crowd. There was no switching on television and watching it, you had to be there in person. The development of instant news through radio and television may account for the gradual fall in the size of crowds at some events, although there are some that still attract huge numbers as people want to say they were there when a certain event took place.

Not only are there events which involve towns or cities, but there are also smaller events which are of importance to families, specific organizations or streets, such as weddings, funerals, church events and street parties at coronations. These too much be classed as events as they are not part of the normal leisure and pleasure round. All too often the recording of these local events tends either to be overlooked or pictorial information does not survive in the public domain. Hence the reason for including one or two of these at the end of this section.

In 1887 Manchester organized a grand exhibition to celebrate the golden jubilee of Queen Victoria's accession to the throne. When Manchester had organized an exhibition in 1857 it was of works of art whereas this exhibition was to stress and publicize the industries of the north-west. However, the exhibition, which lasted throughout the summer of 1887, did include a historical element in that there was a tableau of medieval Manchester. This photograph shows the Market Place as Alfred Darbishire thought it might have looked with the market cross in the centre. The costumes of those on the set exhibit some incongruity in that not only are there medieval costumes but also men in Highland dress, presumably a connection with Bonnie Prince Charlie's passage through Manchester in 1745, and men in Victorian dress. It is to be supposed that this tableau provided a welcome break from the displays of machinery and equipment which made up most of the exhibition.

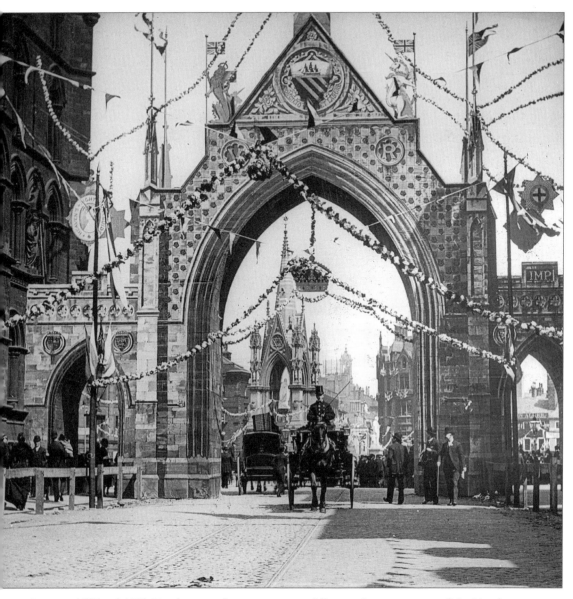

Between 1887 and 1893 Manchester and its citizens were following the construction of the Manchester Ship Canal, intended to link the centre of the English cotton industry with the sea. Although the canal came into full use on 1 January 1894, it was not until 21 May 1894 that it was officially opened by Queen Victoria. The streets were decorated for the occasion and many thousands of people came into the city to see the Queen and admire the decorations. This photograph shows one of several triumphal arches which were erected along the Queen's route from London Road station to No. 1 Dock. It is located at the junction of Albert Square and Mount Street and was similar to one erected at the junction of Cross Street and Albert Square, which can just be seen in the background. Across Deansgate the fire service erected two ladders to form an arch, which was lined with firemen when the Queen passed under it.

It had been hoped that a member of the royal family would have cut the first sod to mark the start of the construction of the Manchester Ship Canal, but this was not to be. When the work was completed Queen Victoria was invited to officially open the Ship Canal. The day set for the official opening was 21 May 1894. The Queen arrived at London Road station at 4.30 p.m. and made her way to Manchester Docks along Market Street, Cross Street, Albert Square, Oxford Street and Stretford Road. On her arrival in Albert Square she was presented with an address of loyalty by the Lord Mayor. This photograph shows the royal carriage in front of the Town Hall with Queen Victoria's head just visible. She appears to be looking at the Albert Memorial, which had been especially restored for the occasion and, at her specific request, left undecorated.

In order that the general public might see the decorations erected for the royal visit in 1894 and celebrate the official opening of the Manchester Ship Canal, the city council decided to ban all but essential traffic from the centre of Manchester on 21 May. It was probably a wise decision as many thousands of people flocked into the centre of Manchester to line the route of the royal procession. This photograph shows a couple in their Sunday best walking through Albert Square during the day, obviously enjoying the day off work and seeing the sights and decorations.

Queen Victoria died on 26 January 1901 and although it had been expected it still sent shock waves through towns and villages. For the first time since 1837 the Lord Mayor had to proclaim a new monarch, Edward VII. On the Sunday after Queen Victoria's funeral memorial services were held in cathedrals and churches throughout the country. In Manchester the Lord Mayor led the official mourning at the service. In this photograph the Lord Mayor, Thomas Briggs, is seen in procession leaving the Town Hall for the Cathedral accompanied by members of the council and other civic dignitaries. The mace, which preceded the Lord Mayor, has black ribbon attached to it.

When Queen Victoria celebrated her diamond jubilee in 1897 Manchester decided to mark the occasion by the erection of a statue in Piccadilly, but before the work could be completed the Queen had died. The statue, designed by Onslow Ford, was paid for by donations from the general public. Lord Roberts was invited to unveil the statue, which was placed in the centre of Piccadilly Esplanade. The unveiling took place on 10 October 1901, exactly fifty years after Queen Victoria had first visited Manchester. The unveiling ceremony, shown here, was attended by large crowds who used every possible angle to get a good view of events. Unfortunately the ceremony was marred by public disorder as grandstands erected for the privileged blocked the view of the general public, with the result that there was much pushing to try and obtain a good view. After the ceremony was over the invited guests had difficulty in getting away so great was the crush.

In 1905 the Manchester Ship Canal Company completed a new dock, No. 9 Dock, intended to accommodate the largest vessels then afloat. Edward VII was invited to open the new dock on 13 July 1905. He arrived at London Road station and travelled through the streets of Manchester to the site of the new dock to officially open it. This photograph shows the royal procession as it passes through Piccadilly on its way to the docks.

Edward VII made a second visit to Manchester in 1909 to officially open the new Manchester Royal Infirmary. The streets were decorated for the occasion and on the actual day of the visit, 6 July 1909, large crowds gathered to cheer him on his way. This photograph shows part of the route with buildings decorated with flags and barriers erected at the edge of the pavements to keep the crowds of spectators back.

In July 1913 George V visited Manchester. On his arrival at London Road station the King was welcomed to Manchester by the Lord Mayor, Alderman Samuel Royse, after which the King travelled to Platt Fields where he was greeted by Manchester's schoolchildren. From Platt Fields he went to the Town Hall, where, after inspecting an honour guard drawn from 2nd Battalion, the Manchester Regiment, he knighted the Lord Mayor on the steps.

Although the death of George V was expected it still came as a surprise to people and the news only spread slowly among the population. The uncertainty about the proclamation of the Prince of Wales as Edward VIII only served to heighten the confusion. Eventually on 22 January 1936 the Lord Mayor proclaimed Edward VIII as the new king from the steps of the Town Hall in front of a crowd estimated to be between 2,000 and 3,000 people. This photograph shows the crowd listening to the proclamation, which was also read in Piccadilly, at New Cross and at All Saints.

After his abdication Edward VIII was succeeded by his brother George VI, whose coronation took place in 1937. Not only were the streets decorated for the occasion as this picture shows, but public buildings were floodlit by night. On the day of the coronation the service was broadcast, but this did not stop events being organized in the city. A special service was held in the cathedral and open air services were organized for Heaton Park, Platt Fields and Wythenshawe Park. Bands also played in the various parks and in central Manchester. Special events were organized for ex-servicemen, children and pensioners. The children of Manchester each received a decorated tin of chocolates, a fountain pen or a souvenir book. At night an illuminated tramcar toured the city and firework displays were held in Heaton Park and Platt Fields. As well as the official events there were also many local events, such as street parties in which all the residents participated.

In 1952 George VI died and was succeeded by his daughter, Elizabeth II. Just as at other coronations public transport vehicles were decorated and toured the streets of the city. Whereas for previous coronations tramcars had been used the chassis of a bus was decorated for the coronation of Elizabeth II in 1953. As with other coronations this century street parties were held as well as officially sponsored events, but one thing made all the difference, the television. For the first time people at home could see events as they happened.

On 24 May 1901 the Manchester Volunteers returned home from active service in the Boer War. Each man received a bounty of £5 for his efforts and, after a parade at Ashton Barracks, travelled to Manchester for a civic reception. The company arrived at London Road station where they were welcomed by the Lord Mayor, Sir James Hoy, and then they marched through the densely packed streets to Manchester Cathedral, where a service was held. The final event of the day was lunch at the Town Hall. The men, who were described as 'grave thin and ill-looking', were apparently wearing khaki rather than the traditional red coats which had been associated with the British army. The *Manchester Guardian* commented that it was a short procession and 'had practically nothing of that bright colour which all healthy Englishmen like to see'. This picture shows the men lined up outside the Town Hall, presumably after returning from the Cathedral.

In 1938 Manchester celebrated the centenary of its incorporation with an exhibition at City Hall on Liverpool Road, which showed different aspects of local government work, a civic banquet and a service at Manchester Cathedral. The celebrations also included a royal visit in that George VI visited the city to officially open the Town Hall Extension. As its contribution to the celebrations Allied Newspapers organized a banquet at the Midland Hotel, shown here, which was attended by distinguished Mancunians and others, including Lord Kelmley and David Lloyd George, who was born in Manchester.

David Lloyd George was born in 1863 in a house in New York Place, Chorlton-on-Medlock. He was destined to become Britain's prime minister for the last two years of the First World War. Lloyd George only lived in Manchester for six weeks before his parents moved from the city. However, Manchester did not forget the connection when they honoured him in September 1918 by bestowing on him the Freedom of the City of Manchester. The ceremony took place not in the Town Hall as normal, but in the Hippodrome on Oxford Street as this could seat a larger audience. This photograph shows the platform party – Lloyd George is the person standing on the left. After the ceremony a civic lunch was held at the Midland Hotel which was followed by an inspection of a guard of honour in Albert Square. Lloyd George's visit to Manchester had to be curtailed because during the day he developed a severe cold.

Britain's second wartime leader of the twentieth century, Winston Churchill, was also honoured with the Freedom of Manchester in 1943. Like Lloyd George, he had connections with the city in that he was the Liberal MP for Manchester North West between 1906 and 1908. During the Second World War Churchill was the last politician to make a speech from the platform of the Free Trade Hall before it was destroyed in the blitz. In 1945 Churchill launched his general election campaign during a visit to Manchester at which it was estimated he was seen by crowds in the region of 80,000. This photograph shows Churchill speaking to the crowds from his car in Piccadilly, together with his wife. In the background is Lewis's shop.

In 1917 Manchester bestowed the Freedom of the City on General Smuts of South Africa. At the same time the Canadian and New Zealand prime ministers were granted the same honour. Two years later General Smuts returned to Manchester where he saw some of the city's historic sites, including Chetham's Hospital. Chetham's had been established as the result of a bequest from a textile merchant, Humphrey Chetham, who died in 1653. The school did not set its sights on sending the boys to Oxford or Cambridge as Manchester Grammar School did, but to provide them with a practical education up to the age of fourteen and then apprentice them to a master who would train them in a useful trade. A visit to the school was on the itinerary of most distinguished visitors to Manchester. General Smuts was no exception, and is seen here being shown round by one of the boys in the school's traditional costume. Today, Chetham's School still occupies the same buildings as it did when it was founded and specializes in music education. It should not be forgotten that as well as the school Humphrey Chetham left money to establish Europe's first free library, Chetham's Library, which occupies premises within the school. It was in this library that Karl Marx and Frederick Engels first met in the 1840s.

Some events are more personal than others. For example, a wedding only directly involves the family and friends of the bride and groom, but often local people would turn out to watch if it was someone with whom they were acquainted. As with visits of royalty and other dignitaries, it broke the daily round. This photograph shows a wedding at Wellington Street Baptist Chapel in June 1914. All that is known about the families involved is that one of them is named Wainwright. It is possible that the gentleman sitting on the right is Joel Wainwright, who died in 1916 aged eighty-five. Wainwright was the author and illustrator of *Memories of Marple* as well as being a prominent accountant, member of the Manchester Field Naturalists, member of the Manchester Geographic Society and a member of the International Decimal Society. The dress in this wedding photograph certainly gives the impression of a society wedding.

One of the most important events in the calendar for Mancunians was the annual Whit Walks. The first
Whit Walk was held in 1801 when it was felt that the children attending the Sunday schools organized by
the Church of England should attend the parish church at least once a year. The early processions started
from St Ann's Square and walked to the Collegiate Church, which was the parish church of Manchester,
to hear divine service and afterwards to have a glass of milk and a bun. When the first walk was held
1,800 Sunday school scholars took part, but gradually the number rose. By 1834 it had reached 4,000 and
by 1901 there were 25,661 children from forty-five Sunday schools taking part. As the numbers grew it
was necessary to find a new starting spot. In 1877 the Whit Walks started for the first time from Albert
Square and made their way along Princess Street, Mosley Street and Market Street to the Cathedral. The
Whit Walks were the one occasion when all the children taking part had new clothes; it was considered to
be a disgrace if a child did not have new clothes for the walks. This photograph shows some of the small
girls taking part in the walk early in the twentieth century. It was taken by Mr Banks, a well-known local
photographer, near the junction of Princess Street and Mosley Street.

Another view of the Whit Walks, taken by Banks from a similar position. Whether it was the same year is
not clear as the weather here appears to be wet with one participant carrying a rain coat. This time Banks
has captured some of the adults who took part: clergy, wardens and sidesmen as well as Sunday school
teachers and probably some parents as well.

A major landmark in the life of all Roman Catholics is their confirmation. This photograph was taken outside St Edmund's Church, Miles Platting on the occasion of a visit by Bishop John Vaughan, Auxiliary Bishop of Salford, for a confirmation service in 1909. John Vaughan was the brother of Herbert Vaughan who was the Bishop of Salford from 1871 to 1892 before becoming Archbishop of Westminster. St Edmund's Church was established as a chapel of ease in 1871 and became a full parish in 1877, the church being completed in 1896. It was situated in one of the poorer parts of Manchester, surrounded by rows of terraced houses. The procession approaching the church has certainly attracted a crowd, but how many of them actually went to the service is not recorded.

As the population of Ardwick grew the Church of England felt that there was a need for a new church to be built. Through the generosity of the Bennett family a site was donated by the family, who also offered to pay for the building as well. The new church, dedicated to St Benedict, was consecrated in 1880 and from the beginning was associated with the Anglo-Catholic wing of the Church of England. This photograph was taken during the period when the Revd William Kemp was Rector of St Benedict's between 1911 and 1941, probably during the 1920s. The note on the reverse of the card describes it as the 'Patronal Festival' which appears to involve a procession of the members of the church through the parish with the wardens carrying the staves, followed by the clergy and then the banners of various church organizations behind. The procession appears to have attracted a large crowd of onlookers, many of whom would have come into contact with Kemp, who worked constantly for those who lived in the parish.

In 1876 the annual Manchester fair was held for the last time on Liverpool Road. The fair, which had been held since 1222, had been moved to Liverpool Road in 1823 and merged with the Bridgewater fair, which had come into existence in 1764 to celebrate the completion of the Bridgewater Canal through to Manchester. By the 1870s the fair, which was held at Easter, had expanded so that it blocked Liverpool Road for about a week and caused traffic congestion along Deansgate. In 1876 the council decided to abolish it as it had become regarded as a nuisance. When this photograph was taken the fair was being staged at Pomona Gardens, but it lasted there for only one year, 1877.

A group of morris dancers entertain shoppers in Piccadilly. In the background is Woolworths store, opened in 1926 on the site of the Albion Hotel.

These rather spectacular floral arches have been erected across Hunt's Bank in readiness for the visit of Edward VII in 1909 to open the new Manchester Royal Infirmary. The building on the right is the office block which formed the headquarters of the Lancashire and Yorkshire Railway.

LEISURE & PLEASURE

In 1833 J.P. Kay commented that 'At present the whole population of Manchester is without any season of recreation, and is ignorant of all amusements, except that very small proportion which frequent the theatre. Healthful exercise in the open air is seldom or never taken by the citizens of this town . . . one reason for this state of the people is that all scenes of interest are remote from this town. . . .' Two years later de Tocqueville commented that in Manchester 'you will never hear the clatter of hoofs when the rich drive back home or are out on pleasure; never the happy shouts of people enjoying themselves nor the harmonious sounds of musical instruments heralding a holiday. You will never see well-dressed people strolling out at leisure . . . or going to the surrounding countryside.'

These two quotations paint a bleak picture of the facilities which were available to Mancunians who wanted to enjoy themselves in the first half of the nineteenth century. Events like royal visits were one thing, but these were infrequent. Working people required other facilities where they could spend their leisure time when they were not working other than in the beer house or the pub. This became all the more pressing when Saturday half-holiday was introduced in the mid-nineteenth century. Some railway companies responded to the closure of warehouses on Saturday afternoons by offering special trips into the surrounding countryside while closer to the centre of Manchester parks began to be established, which provided the opportunity to walk in the 'fresh' air, although until the 1870s many of the parks lacked recreational facilities such as tennis courts, bowling greens and so on, and certainly did not include facilities for children.

Entertainment was also an important part of the leisure-time activities of Mancunians. There were many theatres and music halls in the city which offered a wide range of entertainment from song and dance routines to 'heavy drama'. As well as theatres and music halls there were also musical events in the city. The Gentlemen's Concert Society was the oldest of the organizations which gave concerts, but after 1858 there was the Hallé Orchestra providing regular concerts of classical music while Mr de Jong's concerts tended to concentrate on 'lighter' music. Concerts in the parks attracted large crowds and were popular with brass and military bands.

Another feature of the nineteenth century was the advent of trips to the seaside. It was the development of the railway which helped to popularize the coast, especially places like Blackpool. Factory owners also began to realize that it was better to close the works for a week and undertake the maintenance and repair work than to try and do it with the employees at work. Unlike many of the cotton towns Manchester did not have a specific week when almost everyone left the town. As Manchester was a commercial centre holidays tended to be staggered. In fact, it may be true to say that the Bank Holiday Act of 1870 benefited the workers in the warehouses, shops and offices far more than the man or woman working on the shop floor.

The growth of sporting activities was another feature of the late nineteenth century with Manchester having two football clubs in the Football League by 1900. The playing of football in the streets had been discouraged by the Court Leet as a potential source of disorder. In the 1660s there is even a recorded death of someone by a 'foul' at football. Other sports also made their appearance in the nineteenth century such as cricket, tennis as well as skating, curling and attending the races. These, together with the opening of parks, meant that by 1900 Manchester did have some facilities where people could enjoy themselves after work and on Sundays.

One of the best known places of entertainment in Manchester was Belle Vue. The original pleasure grounds had been established by John Jennison in Adswood, Stockport in 1826, but lack of space for expansion meant that he had to look for an alternative place for his pleasure grounds and small zoo. He chose a thirty-six acre site on Hyde Road, opening there in 1836. After his initial success Jennison ran into financial difficulties, but his creditors gave him time and very quickly he was able to repay his debts well before they fell due. Gradually Belle Vue began to attract a growing number of visitors, helped by the introduction, in 1852, of firework displays based on a theme, such as the Lisbon earthquake or the Afghan wars, which was changed each year. From the beginning Jennison had kept some animals at Belle Vue. As the number of animals increased so did the number of ones from abroad which ultimately resulted in the creation of Belle Vue Zoo. Jennison and his family realized that to be successful, they had to introduce new features each year. For example, the introduction and development of the amusement park fits in with this policy. This photograph, taken after 1908, shows the toboggan run which was introduced in 1908 after James Jennison had seen one at White City in Stretford.

Another feature at Belle Vue was the open-air dance floor, which fronted the firework lake. A wooden dance floor had been introduced in the 1850s and proved to be very popular, a popularity which continued up to the Second World War. Dancing was only one of many activities which were held at Belle Vue. Brass band concerts were introduced in the 1850s, hand bell ringing contests as well as flower shows also featured in the calendar of Belle Vue's annual events. This photograph was taken in the 1930s when Belle Vue was still a popular place for people to visit. Visitors not only came from Manchester, but from many parts of the north of England and the Potteries. There was even a special tram siding constructed at Belle Vue because of the popularity of the place. The largest number ever to visit Belle Vue was on Easter Monday 1944 when around 180,000 crammed into the site. Unfortunately Belle Vue began to decline after the Second World War and was eventually closed; the site was redeveloped in the 1980s.

BELLE VUE CIRCUS
1930

In 1930 Belle Vue added another event to its calendar – the Christmas circus held in the King's Hall. The circus was organized by the same people who organized the circus at Blackpool during the summer. In many respects they were using their talents to provide entertainment for people who would not have travelled to the seaside in mid-winter, but who would visit something nearer home. Each performance could be seen by 7,000 people, there being two performances a day over Christmas. The first circus at Belle Vue included two teams of liberty horses, eight Shetland ponies, five pygmy elephants and several bears performing different tricks. In addition there were the usual clowns, acrobats and human entertainers. This postcard shows the first of Belle Vue's Christmas circuses in 1930.

Belle Vue was one of the few places in Manchester where big events could be staged as it had several large buildings. The use of Belle Vue for exhibitions and other events had the added advantage that there was something else for those attending to do. This photograph shows the fifth annual flower show of the London and North Western Railway Co. (North Eastern Division) held on 17 August 1912. Entrants from the Manchester area competed for the Founders Cup while for those from Yorkshire there was the Yorkshire Cup. Awards for best station gardening and for flowers grown by signalmen in signal-box window boxes were among those given.

The first public parks in Manchester were not opened until 1845 when Philips Park and Queens Park were handed over to Manchester. The money to purchase the land and to lay them out was raised by public subscription while the borough council obtained approval in the 1844 Police Act to expend money on their maintenance. The intention of those who supported the public parks movement was to try and bring something of the countryside into the urban areas. The parks were laid out in a formal manner with walks, flower beds, lawns and ponds or lakes, but no facilities where games could be played. This picture shows the lake and some of the grounds at Philips Park.

After the opening of Philips Park and Queens Park in 1845 it was another twenty-two years before Manchester added any more public open space to its ownership. In 1867 the council took over the five acre Ardwick Green, which had originally been a private park maintained by the residents of the housing fronting it. When it was a private park the area was surrounded by railings and to gain admission you required a key, one being issued to each resident. The main feature of the green was a large pond or lake in the centre, mentioned by Mrs Banks in her novel *The Manchester Man*. When Manchester took over the green the character of the area was changing, the large houses were being replaced and the green being neglected. When they took it over the corporation improved it and added the bandstand which can be seen in the background.

In terms of area covered, nineteenth-century Manchester was relatively small, with few open spaces which were suitable for providing large parks for its citizens. In 1869 the council looked outside its boundaries for land on which to construct a public park. A site was purchased in Moss Side, but it took almost seven years to resolve the difficulties caused by the fact that Moss Side was not part of Manchester at that time. Eventually in 1876 the problems were overcome and Alexandra Park was laid out at a cost of £60,000. Alfred Darbishire, a prominent Manchester architect, designed the lodges at the entrance to the park. The one which is shown here, on Alexandra Road, not only acted as the park superintendent's home, but also as an administrative office. The broad carriageway was intended to enable carriages to drive through the park although few probably did. As with other parks there was a bandstand which attracted large audiences in the summer when local brass bands and bands from the regiments stationed in Manchester performed.

In 1906 the Platt Hall estate was advertised for sale. The original intention was that it should be sold for housing, but it did not find a buyer. A campaign was mounted in Rusholme to encourage the city council to purchase the estate for the public and convert it into a public park. The city council was reluctant to do this, but after a town poll showed there was support for the idea they purchased the estate for £59,875. Much of the land was poorly drained and required major civil engineering works. As there was much unemployment in Manchester at the time it was decided that the unemployed should be given the task of putting in the drains and landscaping the new park. However the work was not done very well and in the end outside contractors had to be brought in to finish the job. The park was opened in 1910 by the lord mayor with a large crowd of people in attendance. This picture shows the 6½ acre boating lake, which was surrounded by a walk of about a mile and in the centre an artificial island where wildlife could breed.

In the inner suburbs of Manchester it was not possible to create parks as the land was too expensive, although these were the areas which needed most public open spaces. In some areas small plots of vacant land were taken over by the council and turned into children's playgrounds with swings, see-saws, roundabouts and slides. Kemp Street playground covered 1¼ acres and cost £12,982 to acquire and lay out. In 1913 the city council embarked on an ambitious scheme to appoint six lady instructors or games leaders to encourage the proper use of the facilities provided. It is possible that one of these instructresses has organized the photographic session as the children look remarkably tidy and organized.

In 1868 the graveyard surrounding St Michael's Church, Angel Meadow, was converted into a playground and area where people could assemble. This was the first of several such conversions during the next seventy years. In 1890, when St Mary's Church off Deansgate was demolished, the site was also landscaped, providing those who worked in the area with a place to go at lunchtime to eat their sandwiches. The difficulty in allowing building on the sites of former churches was that they were surrounded by graveyards. Before any development could take place the bodies would have to be exhumed and re-interred – an expensive operation. In some cases the number of burials exceeded 20,000 as at St John's churchyard on Byrom Street. St John's Church was demolished in 1931. Part of the site was landscaped, but part of it was converted into a playground, shown here, for many of the children who lived in this part of central Manchester.

Towns and cities have always had their street entertainers. Manchester was no exception to this. One of the most popular street entertainers appears to have been the man with the 'dancing bear'. The bears came from Russia and their handlers were probably east Europeans. Dancing bears on the streets disappeared as a result of the First World War.

Street musicians were also a feature of Manchester's streets. Whether this was a barrel organ or a street piano is uncertain as is the exact location of the scene. These instruments could be hired for a few pence and trundled around the streets of Manchester, playing popular tunes of the day. Members of the public would be encouraged to give money to the person turning the handle, thus enabling him to earn a few coppers to support himself and his family. Some of the barrel organs which would have been heard on the streets of Manchester may have been made locally in a factory on Great Ancoats Street, opened in 1894 by Domenico Antonelli. Whether this instrument was made there is not known.

In September 1852 the Manchester Free Library opened in the former Hall of Science in Castlefield. As well as a reference section there was also a lending library, which was well used from the beginning. Gradually the benefits of public libraries became acknowledged and the council began to open branches, often as a result of local demands in areas which would today be regarded as inner city. In some cases these libraries were little more than converted houses, as the one in Hulme was for a number of years. When Manchester absorbed surrounding areas among the services they introduced were lending libraries, but where the authority had introduced a library service it was merged with Manchester's libraries. One district which did not have a library when it became part of Manchester was Chorlton-cum-Hardy, which had been part of Withington Urban District Council. Manchester opened its first library in Chorlton in November 1908 in a converted house, but this was only a temporary measure. A new library was opened in 1914 with a more extensive stock and better facilities. This photograph shows the lending library in Chorlton Library probably in the 1920s. The neatly arranged rows of books and the card catalogue in the background were typical of libraries at this time. The person on the left may be a library assistant carefully straightening the books to ensure they are in the correct order. It is interesting to note that ladies were employed as library assistants in the 1870s as the library could not recruit enough men, especially in the branches. According to one commentator the young ladies were far more helpful and attentive to their duties than their male counterparts and suggested that they should also be employed in the reference library in Manchester as it would improve the service.

Another service which local government
provided was that of bath- and wash-houses.
Swimming baths were also introduced where
members of the public could engage in healthful
exercise and children could be taught to swim.
This photograph shows the Victoria Baths on
Hathersage Road (formerly High Street), which
were opened in 1906 at a cost of £59,000. The
baths were intended to serve the populations of
Rusholme, part of Chorlton Medlock and
Longsight, which were among the most built-up
parts of the city and lacking the facilities found
at the public baths. As well as a swimming pool,
the building included a laundry and a Turkish
bath. Around the side of the pool galleries were
erected so that swimmers could be watched or
events staged whereby spectators could have a
good view of what was going on. These baths
are now closed although attempts are being
made to save them and bring them.

Towards the end of the nineteenth century
several new theatres were built including two
which staged variety shows, the Palace and
the Manchester Hippodrome. Both were
located in Oxford Street, only a few yards
from each other. This photograph shows the
Hippodrome, which was designed by Frank
Matcham for Oswald Stoll. The theatre was
capable of staging music hall, circus or water
spectaculars. It cost about £45,000 and could
seat 3,000 people. Under the stage there
were stables for horses and livestock while
over the auditorium part of the roof could
slide back to increase ventilation. The theatre
opened on Boxing Day 1904 with a show
which made use of all the facilities that the
theatre had at its disposal. This photograph
was taken in 1934 shortly before it closed
and was demolished. The replacement was
the Gaumont Cinemas, which opened in
1936. The name 'Hippodrome' was not lost
to Manchester, but was transferred to the
Ardwick Green Empire, which closed in
1961.

Oxford Street/Peter Street has sometimes been likened to the West End of London as many of Manchester's theatres and places of entertainment were to be found along the two streets or on roads leading from them. Among the theatres which could be found on Oxford Street was the Princes Theatre, a rival to the older Theatre Royal on Peter Street. The Princes Theatre, designed by Edward Salomons, was opened in 1864 by Charles Calvert, a well-known actor-manager. This photograph was taken in 1936 when the Princes Theatre was staging its annual pantomime. During the latter decades of the nineteenth century there was much rivalry between the Princes and the Theatre Royal as to who could stage the most elaborate pantomime, a rivalry which some critics did not like as they claimed that the story was subordinated to the special effects, resulting in the loss of the original idea behind pantomime. The Princes Theatre closed in 1940 and was demolished shortly afterwards.

In November 1922 the first broadcast was made by 2ZY from a small studio in the Metropolitan Vickers Works in Trafford Park. This was the beginning of public service broadcasting in Manchester. The Trafford Park studio was far from adequate and so it was decided to move to the top floor of a warehouse on Dickenson Street and use the chimney of the nearby power station for its aerials. Later the radio station moved to a building off Deansgate, where it had two studios and was able to expand both its output and the type of programmes it could broadcast. In 1928 the BBC, as it now was, moved once more to a newly erected building in Piccadilly, where it stayed until the 1970s, when it moved to New Broadcasting House on Oxford Road. This photograph shows Isobel Baillie (right) and other musicians broadcasting from one of Manchester's studios. Other programmes which were broadcasting in the early days included *Kiddies Corner*, election results and the first full-length drama production, *The Butterfly on the Wheel*.

During the nineteenth century there was a very strong temperance movement centred in Manchester which organized lectures and meetings to try and encourage members of the public to abstain from alcoholic drink. This photograph shows a lunchtime meeting outside a factory gate at which the evils of alcohol were expounded by a speaker. Not all the audience were adults as this photograph shows. There are some at the back of the crowd who are obviously children, but whether they were in employment or not is uncertain. The table in the foreground may have been used when anyone wanted to sign the pledge to give up alcoholic drink.

Two major football clubs have their origins in Manchester – Manchester United and Manchester City. This illustration shows the Manchester United team which won the FA Cup in 1909 when they beat Bristol City 1–0 at Crystal Palace. This was their first major success since their foundation as Newton Heath Lancashire and Yorkshire Railway in 1878. In 1885 the name was shortened to Newton Heath and became Manchester United in 1902. The team played their early matches at North Road, Monsall, before moving in 1893 to Bank Street at Clayton and finally in 1910 to Old Trafford, which is part of Stretford, not Manchester.

Manchester City Football Club was started two years after Newton Heath, in 1880, as West Gorton St Marks, a team attached to a church. In 1887 the West Gorton Club merged with Gorton Athletic to form Ardwick FC which in 1894 became Manchester City FC. In their early years the club had several grounds before settling at Hyde Road in 1887. Manchester City stayed at the Hyde Road ground until 1923 when it moved to its present ground, Maine Road. This photograph shows the team sitting down for lunch sometime during the 1930s.

A large family house in Manchester which is fortunate to have its own tennis court. It is probable that the children would not have been allowed to play on the court, it being reserved for their parents and their guests.

Snow brings the child out in everyone, as these men show by having a snowball fight in the back garden.

SOCIAL CONDITIONS

Between 1772 and 1788 the population of Manchester doubled, reaching over 70,000 by the time the first census was held in 1801. This dramatic increase in population resulted in a huge demand for new housing which was difficult to meet. Houses were erected very quickly with little regard for the sanitary conditions or the density of people per acre. Many of the new houses lacked proper foundations and sanitary facilities. Back-to-back houses abounded in places like Angel Meadow, Ancoats, Hulme and Chorlton-on-Medlock as well as in parts of central Manchester. Cellar dwellings and multi-occupation were also common as the population grew. The problem was that the authorities had no powers to deal with the growing slums, not even adequate building regulations. Clean water was a rarity as was the existence of proper sewers. Sewage was tipped into the rivers and streams as was industrial effluent. In the mid-nineteenth century it was a moot point if you fell into the River Irwell whether you were drowned, poisoned or suffocated. An analysis of the River Medlock in 1845 revealed the presence of chemicals such as chlorine in such large amounts that if they were present in those quantities today the city centre would be evacuated.

The 1844 Police Act made an attempt to improve the situation by insisting that all new property had adequate sanitary facilities, but the act did nothing to tackle the legacy of the previous four decades of bad housing construction. It was not until the council appreciated the need for clean, running water, and the construction of the Longdendale reservoirs to supply this in the 1850s, that steps could be taken to improve things.

By the middle of the nineteenth century the population of central Manchester reached its zenith, over 186,000 people, after which it began to decline. Bodies like the Manchester and Salford Sanitary Association began to draw attention to the slums and the condition of those who lived in them. The removal of some of the slums began, not as a result of sanitary legislation but as a result of the demands of commerce, industry and transport for land on which to expand. For instance, the construction of Central station in the 1870s resulted in removal of several thousand people from the area, many of whom lived in poor quality housing.

It was not until after the First World War that local authorities were able to start programmes of slum clearance. At first the levels of council housing were restricted, but gradually the number of houses they were allowed to build was increased. The new house building programme, however, resulted in an increase in the outward growth of the town and the development of what would be called 'green field sites'. Often these sites were to be found between major routes into the city which had been ignored by private developers. The programme of slum clearance continued into the 1950s and 1960s with overspill estates, the expansion of Wythenshawe and the building of system-built houses and flats, the latter proving so disastrous that they have now been demolished and replaced by traditional housing.

For those who lived in the slums of Victorian and Edwardian Manchester there were organizations devoted to help them. Organizations like the Manchester and Salford Methodist Mission, the Manchester City Mission and Wood Street Mission were successful in helping many of those who were in difficulties. For those who could not, or would not, seek help from the voluntary bodies there was always the 'parish' or the workhouse, which was really the last resort.

For those who fell ill there were hospitals and dispensaries. The main hospital was the Manchester Royal Infirmary, but there were several specialist hospitals in nineteenth-century Manchester such as the eye hospital, the skin hospital and St Mary's Lying-in Hospital. In the poorer parts there were organizations like the Chorlton Dispensary at All Saints and the Ancoats and Ardwick Dispensary. Sometimes the charitable organizations provided help, such as the nurses employed by the Manchester and Salford Methodist Mission, who were said to be very highly regarded by the residents of Ancoats and trusted far more than doctors.

Until the late nineteenth century this court, known as Bakehouse Court, stood behind the buildings on Long Millgate facing Manchester Grammar School. The properties were probably built in the fifteenth or sixteenth centuries when Long Millgate was a main route out of the town. Originally the houses would have fronted the road, but as the population expanded so the gardens were built over and cottages erected. Gradually the standard of the area declined so that by the late nineteenth century many of the buildings required urgent structural work as well as other improvements to make them habitable. This is clearly obvious from the building on the right which is held up by timber beams not only at the gable end, but also to adjacent properties. These cottages were timber-framed and at least one of the buildings on the site was cruck-framed. As a result of redevelopment in the late nineteenth century these buildings were demolished. Within a hundred years even their replacements have disappeared and the site is now a car park.

Further along Long Millgate, in a bend in the River Irk, stood Gibraltar which was in a very poor state by the time this photograph was taken. The timber-framed house in the centre was built, according to the date over the door, in 1654 when the area would have been surrounded by open country and the river full of fish. By 1852/3 those inspecting the area for the Manchester and Salford Sanitary Association were recommending that the buildings be demolished. Many were in multi-occupation and in need of urgent works. In some cases there were five or six people living in a room. It was not until the end of the century that something was done and the buildings cleared away.

One of the worst areas of poor quality housing was Angel Meadow which lay between Rochdale Road and the River Irk. The area had started to develop in the late eighteenth century as Manchester expanded, and by the mid-nineteenth century back-to-back houses and courts abounded. The main road leading into Angel Meadow was Angel Street, photographed here in the 1890s. This was the widest street in the district with three-storeyed houses lining it. These houses may have started out as houses with workshops on the top floor, but by the time this photograph was taken some of them had been converted into lodging houses. These houses were probably built in about 1800, each having a cellar which, although railed off, probably housed a family. Note the rather nice Georgian door cases which were to be found in many parts of Manchester. It was said that the only person who did not live in the area who could enter safely was the midwife, while the police were said to patrol in twos and threes.

This rather tumble-down block of buildings was known as Parsonage Buildings and located at St Mary's Parsonage, behind Deansgate and close to St Mary's Church. Although today it is an area of offices, in the nineteenth century there were several hat manufactories, a brass and copper works and a mill backing on to the river. Other industrial sites in the area including a fustian and cotton stiffening works, a coach manufactory and a cotton finishing works. Gradually these factories disappeared as did the church in 1890, the site of the church and the churchyard being landscaped.

During the 1890s there were several schemes to try and improve living conditions for the residents of Ancoats. One of the more ingenious schemes was the conversion of a former cotton mill on Jersey Street. The work involved dividing the building cross-ways so that each flat or tenement had three rooms, two with outside walls and natural light while the third room, in the centre, had no natural light at all. Each flat was provided with running water in the living room, but there were no individual toilets, each floor having its own. During the years between the wars it was reported that Jersey Street dwellings became the home of several of the gangs which were to be found in the Ancoats area. During the Second World War it was said that the elderly people who lived there felt safter in the inner rooms of their flats than in an air-raid shelter. Eventually they were evacuated because the size of the mill made it an obvious target. The mill was demolished after the war.

In 1892 Manchester sponsored a competition to design a tenement block in which to rehouse some of the people who lived in the New Cross area. One of the entrants was Thomas Worthington who included bathrooms in his scheme, a proposal which was greeted with scepticism by some who said the residents would use the baths to keep coal in. The winners were Spalding and Cross, who designed the building shown here. Each flat had its own water supply and toilet with a balcony which overlooked a court yard. A contemporary account described the block as 'of fair, average character, light and airy'. At street level shops were provided to replace some of those which had been demolished when the area was cleared for Victoria Square. The block has recently been refurbished and is used as sheltered housing for elderly people.

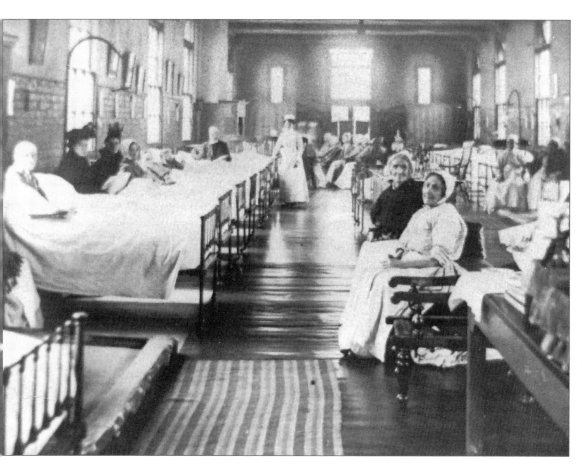

In 1834 the old Elizabethan Poor Law was amended and a new system of Poor Law Unions established. Central Manchester together with Cheetham and Ancoats constituted the Manchester Union while all the districts between the rivers Medlock and Mersey became part of the Chorlton Union. Districts to the north of Manchester which eventually became part of the city were included in the Prestwich Union. Each union had its own workhouse and officials. The Manchester workhouse was originally located on New Bridge Street, on a site which was later to be absorbed by Victoria station. The Chorlton Union initially used a workhouse in Hulme, but this soon proved to be inadequate and so was moved to a new site in Withington, which cost £180 per acre and where there was sufficient room for expansion. The workhouse opened in 1855 and hospital wards were added between 1860 and 1868, designed by Thomas Worthington and based on the recommendations of Florence Nightingale. This photograph taken in about 1900 shows one of the female wards in the hospital part of Withington Workhouse.

When the census for the workhouse is examined it is surprising how few staff are recorded as being present on census night. Some of those were what could be called today members of the management team, including the master and matron as well as the porter and teaching staff. Although the workhouse had around 1,300 inmates there were still only about twenty nurses. It is possible that a number of staff went into the workhouse each day and lived in the surrounding area, although the census does not reveal who they were. It is possible that a lot of the work around the workhouse was done by the inmates themselves as a wide range of occupations was represented from labourers to laundresses and, in 1871, a curate of the established church. Although workhouses were detested, as they separated husbands and wives and children, it has also to be borne in mind that the conditions they might have been living in outside the workhouse would have been terrible. The children did receive some education and may have been better educated than their counterparts outside. By the beginning of the twentieth century, diets for the inmates were published in the Union's yearbook. It was not very exciting with breakfast and tea being the same, although dinner did vary each day. The most interesting fact that can be gleaned from these dietary tables is that one group had ½lb of rice pudding, sago pudding or bread pudding just before going to bed! This photograph, taken at the same time as the previous one, shows some of the male inmates in what appears to be a workshop.

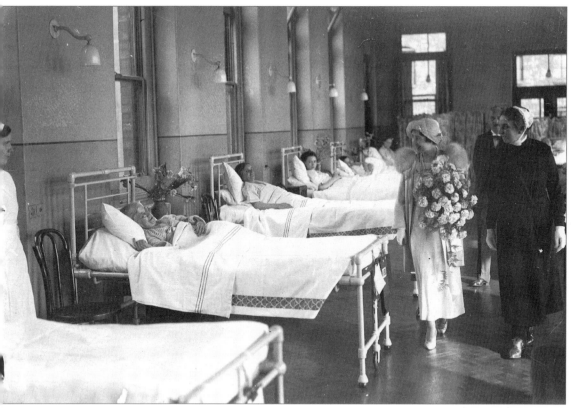

In 1828 the Ardwick and Ancoats Dispensary was established at No. 181 Great Ancoats Street to provide help for those who lived in this densely populated part of Manchester. In the first years the dispensary dealt with 1,108 home patients and outpatients together with 169 accident cases. As the demands made on the dispensary grew so it was necessary to find larger premises, which it did at Ancoats Cresent, opposite Every Street. However in 1870 this site was purchased by the Midland Railway and the dispensary had to move again. This time a site was found on Mill Street and the nucleus of Ancoats Hospital was built and opened as a proper hospital in 1879. Demand for beds always outstripped availability because of the area it was located in and the large number of factory accidents. By the 1880s these exceeded 3,500 per annum and continued to grow. This photograph shows the Duchess of York (later to be Queen Elizabeth when her husband, George VI, became king) visiting in 1932. Note the lack of privacy with no curtains, or even provision for curtains, around each bed.

In 1916 the British Red Cross acquired Grangethorpe House on the borders of Rusholme and Fallowfield and converted it into an orthopaedic hospital for men who had been injured during the fighting in France and elsewhere. The house was built in 1882, probably for a merchant and his family. This photograph is captioned and gives the date of Christmas 1917. It shows the wards decorated for the event together with some of the nurses. In 1929 the building was acquired first by the Manchester Royal Infirmary and then by Manchester High School for Girls in 1929.

In September 1910 Manchester opened a hostel for women on a site at Red Bank. Mary Ashton House, as it was called, was a continuation of Sir William Crossley's housing experiment which had already resulted in a men's lodging house being erected. This new hostel, designed by the city architect, cost £13,000 and was open for inspection by the police at any time of the day or night. It was said that the hostel combined a firm but humane management of the 222 women who could be accommodated in their own cubicles. In addition to sleeping accommodation the building also included a recreation room, kitchen on the ground floor and a wash-house, shown here, with baths and lockers in the basement.

Wood Street Mission was founded by Alfred Alsop in 1869 in premises on Lombard Street, moving to Wood Street in 1873. The area where Alsop worked was described by a police officer as 'the rendezvous of thieves and a very hot bed of social iniquity and vice'. Alsop's original aim was to relieve need 'whether spiritual, physical or mental'. Meals were served to the hungry and clogs and clothing given away to those who needed them. Seaside trips for children and Christmas treats became a feature of Wood Street. As social attitudes and requirements changed the Wood Street Mission adapted its activities to meet the changing demand. As well as relieving the needy the Mission took on an educative role, such as the one shown here where girls are being taught first aid.

In the slums of Manchester much work was done by various charitable and religious organizations. For example, the Manchester City Mission was associated with the Church of England while the Methodists established the Manchester and Salford Methodist Mission to work in the slums of the city. The Methodist Mission was started in 1886 when the Methodist Central Hall on Oldham Street was rebuilt. This photograph, taken between the wars, shows coal being delivered to a resident of poor quality housing in Manchester. In the background washing can be seen hanging across the road, indicating that the delivery is taking place in an area of back-to-back housing. The hanging of washing across the road was forbidden in the 1844 Police Act and those breaking the law could be fined up to 40s.

The Manchester and Salford Methodist Mission was very much a 'doing' organization. Its staff were prepared to go out into the streets of Ancoats and Hulme to being help and assistance to all who needed it irrespective of their religious persuasion. They met prisoners being discharged from Strangeways Prison and offered them assistance. They also provided accommodation for men coming into Manchester seeking work who did not want to stay in one of the many lodging houses in the city centre. In order to pay for their accommodation those men who did not have work would chop firewood, sell it, whitewash buildings and do other work arranged by the Mission. For women who sought assistance help was also available from the Mission in the form of a refuge as well as a coffee tavern, shown here, and a servants' registry was even maintained. In addition to services the Mission also provided some basic medical help for the residents of the poorer parts of Manchester, those using it often preferring the advice of the sisters to that of doctors.

Another organization involved in helping the needy was the Salvation Army. During the Depression in the 1930s the Salvation Army ran soup kitchens to provide some food for those in need. This photograph shows one such soup kitchen where those recipients are being fed. According to the labels on the canisters and on the van, rice, peas, beans and potatoes form the basic diet. It may not have been a scientifically balanced diet, but for hungry people it was sustenance which they gratefully accepted.

Another picture of the Salvation Army in the 1930s providing food for the needy of Manchester. What is in the bucket is not clear, but it is certainly hot as steam can be seen rising from it. It appears as if priority is being given to the children with their small basins while the adults are holding jugs.

In complete contrast to the conditions which were found in central Manchester, where population densities could be as high as 400 or 500 people per acre, this family lived in the leafy suburbs, away from the overcrowding and unhygienic conditions of areas like Ancoats. This photograph was taken in the front garden, as houses on the opposite side of the road can just be seen in the background.

Another family group showing the ladies of the house and the children. Their dress contrasts with that of the children shown in other pictures in this section, and the ones in Section Eight.

CHILDREN

According to the Concise Oxford Dictionary childhood is the 'time from childbirth to puberty', one of the few events in life that everyone experiences. Although this definition appears to be satisfactory it must be remembered that there have been and still are cultures, and periods of history, where childhood ends before puberty, and others where it technically carries on for a number of years afterwards. In this section childhood has been assumed to end when the child leaves school.

What is known about childhood, especially that of last generations, depends on people's recollections being recorded in some form or other. Much is only known from hearsay or legend. Everyone has had a different experience of childhood, and there will even be variations depending on which part of the country a child grew up in.

Although people recall their childhood memories, often it is through 'rose-coloured spectacles' – 'the summers seemed longer and sunnier and winters snowier'. Photographs are one way of helping to recall childhood in some cases and enhance a person's sketchy recollections. Sometimes people in old age will see a photograph which will remind them of something they have done or been involved with and pass the information on. Sometimes they can add information relating to a picture which brings it to life. Often people do not think anyone will be interested in what they did as children and are pleasantly surprised when someone does express interest.

This final section of the book is devoted entirely to photographs of children from Manchester. If some could speak they would reveal that they have seen a great many changes not only in the face of the city, but also in the way we live and do things. When these children were photographed radio and television had not made their appearance, while moving pictures were just beginning to flicker across the screen. Again in the field of transport, railways and trams were supreme while cars were noisy and unreliable.

Children are the future generation and lifeblood of any settlement. If there are no children the community dies out. What these children did in their lives will have helped to shape the succeeding and future generations, not only of their own families but of life in Manchester generally. The more recollections that we have from children the better our understanding of what life was like in the past, and 'flesh and bones' are added to the skeleton of facts.

Manchester High School for Girls was founded in 1874 'to provide for Manchester's daughters what has been provided without stint for Manchester's sons'. When it was founded in Portland Place it was regarded as a pioneer in the education of girls. In 1880 the school moved to Dover Street where it remained until 1929 when it moved to Grangethorpe House. The old house was replaced by a new school building which was destroyed in 1940. In 1951 a new school building was opened on the site. This photograph shows the girls packing parcels, but the note at the back does not explain for whom they are intended. The building in which the photograph was taken was the one at Dover Street, now part of Manchester University.

Ardwick Higher Grade School was opened in 1894 on Devonshire Street. Later, in 1909, Manchester Education Committee introduced a new policy whereby facilities were made available for children who could stay on at school above the minimum leaving age. The schools which were to cater for these children were to be called central schools. Rather than build new schools several existing schools were renamed, including Ardwick Higher Grade School which was sometimes referred to as Devonshire Higher Grade School. One well-known pupil who attended Ardwick Higher Grade School was Ellen Wilkinson, also known as Red Ellen. She went on to become a Manchester city councillor and later MP for Middlesbrough East and Minister of Education in the first Atlee government in 1945. Another well-known person who attended the same school was Frederick James Marquis, later Lord Woolton, who was not only a pupil at the school but also a pupil-teacher there as well. Unfortunately this picture of one of the classes at the school in the inter-war years gives no indication of which class it was or the date, only the name of the school.

This group of children came from St Andrew's School on Homer Street in Ancoats and was probably taken at Mayfield baths. St Andrew's School was founded in 1836 as St Andrew's Infant and Sunday School and gradually extended over the next two decades until by 1860 it was a two-storeyed building with three entrances. The school lost many pupils in the 1870s when Ancoats Goods Depot was built, a problem which was to occur again in the twentieth century. It is interesting to note that as early as 1871 the school was having photographs of its pupils taken, so this one is one of a long series of school photographs from St Andrew's School. However, only a few appear to have survived. The school buildings were eventually demolished at the same time as the church, in about 1961.

From its earliest days Manchester free libraries appreciated the importance of providing facilities for children in its libraries. Reading rooms for boys and girls were included when new libraries were built. This photograph shows children sitting at tables in the Chester Road Library in Hulme between the wars. Chester Road children's room was established in the late nineteenth century and was very popular from the time it opened.

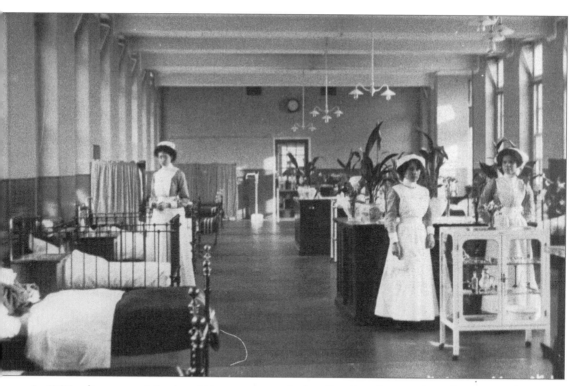

In 1790 a disagreement developed between the medical staff at the infirmary about the treatment of children and women with gynaecological problems. Several doctors, led by Dr Charles White, left the infirmary and established St Mary's Lying-in Hospital in premises on Quay Street. During the next 100 years the hospital occupied several different buildings in the Quay Street and Salford areas. In 1892 St Mary's moved to a new hospital at the corner of Gloucester Street (now Whitworth Street West) and Oxford Street, but in 1904 the hospital merged with the Southern Hospital for Women and Children. In 1911 a new hospital was opened on High Street (now Hathersage Road) in Chorlton-on-Medlock, but the one in central Manchester was retained as it was felt that there was a need for such facilities in the area. This photograph shows one of the wards at the High Street Hospital where the staff concentrated on babies and gynaecological problems. At the side of each bed there is a cot while the staff, in their starched uniforms, stand by a cabinet containing medicines.

This group of children was photographed in about 1904 in Rusholme with a leading Rusholme resident, William Royle. Why he had gathered them together is not recorded, but the existence of a garland, held aloft by one of the children, suggests that it might have been a May Day celebration organized by Royle for the people of Rusholme.

At a time when the ambition of every little boy was to be an engine driver, this boy and a girl, presumably his sister, are trying out this motor car for size. It is not possible to identify the make of car, but it is worth noting that Manchester did have a car industry in the early twentieth century. The early Rolls-Royce cars were made in Hulme, while between 1910 and 1929 Ford cars were made in Trafford Park and Belsize cars were made in Clayton.

It is not known who this little boy is or whereabouts in Manchester he was photographed. The photograph, which was almost certainly posed, gives a good indication of the type of dress boys were wearing at the beginning of the twentieth century, including a waistcoat. Despite the fact that he is bare-footed the boy seems cheerful enough.

This is a scene which must have been repeated countless times throughout the north-west, donkey stoning the steps and pavement in front of the house. Donkey stones, obtained from the ironmonger or more likely from rag and bone men, were made on the ground mixed with additives such as dolly blue. The result was a door step which looked white or cream when freshly completed. Although donkey stoning was usually done by the woman of the house on this occasion a boy appears to be doing it, but for what reason it is not known.

One must wonder what these three boys were talking about or what mischief they were planning. These must have been halcyon days for the three before they left school and started work in the local mill or factory. Once they left school the opportunity to sit and exchange stories would have disappeared, and so would their childhood.

One of the events of the year for children who were associated with the Wood Street Mission was the annual visit to the seaside for the week. The children were taken by train to Ainsdale where they camped close to the sea and spent a week under canvas. The cost of the visit was met from donations with a small contribution from the parents. Once at Ainsdale the camp was visited by local dignitaries such as the mayor and other leading citizens of the town. This photograph shows the girls, all smartly dressed in smocks for the photographer, lining up outside the mission's premises on Wood Street in central Manchester. If you look on the left hand side of the photograph you can just see the boys waiting for their turn to be photographed.

Christmas time was always eagerly awaited by the children and adults associated with Wood Street Mission. The provision of Christmas treats was established in the nineteenth century and continued into the present century. Those who benefited were the poor and needy, but by the twentieth century the work of the Mission covered the whole city and not just the small area around Wood Street. This photograph of the inter-war years shows the Lord Mayor of Manchester and the officials of the Mission awaiting the arrival of Father Christmas with a crowd of children, who appear to be oblivious of the gentleman in red, who is probably standing on the fire escape.

ACKNOWLEDGEMENTS

Over the years a large number of photographs have been taken of Manchester and its suburbs. Although there were photographers taking them in the decades between 1850 and 1890 it is to members of the Manchester Amateur Photographic Society that historians must be grateful, for it was from that body that the first attempt was made to photographically record Manchester for posterity. From then on, until the 1970s, the Record Section of MAPS recorded, at the behest of the Manchester Local History Library, many of the streets and buildings of Manchester, buildings and streets which have since disappeared. As well as members of MAPS there are many other local photographers who have helped to preserve a photographic image of Manchester, its buildings and its events. Some early ones were James Mudd, W. Fischer and A. Brothers, while others like Samuel Coulthurst and R. Banks were working at the end of the nineteenth and beginning of the twentieth century using newly developed cameras and films. Nor should the work of the City Engineers Department be overlooked for from the late 1890s cameras became part of their equipment. Photographs of many of their major projects were recorded as well as general views of streets when such illustrations were required for reports to council committees. Another important group who deserve thanks are the press photographers and the thousands of photographs they took not only of events, but general scenes like people at work. They too add to our knowledge of what Manchester looked like in the past. We should remember to thank the postcard producers of the late nineteenth and early twentieth century for the vast number of cards they produced, not only of buildings but also of street scenes and scenes in the suburbs of Manchester. Many of these were not nationally known postcard publishers, but small local people, often newsagents. My thanks are due to all these photographers and postcard publishers for their dedication and work. Without them such books would be impossible to compile.

My thanks are also due to Manchester Public Libraries and in particular the Local History Library, now the Local Studies Department, for their work in collecting and preserving so many photographs. My thanks are due to the staff there, in particular David Taylor, for their help over the years when researching for this and other books.

I also wish to thank Ted Gray, Airviews (Manchester), Salford Archives Department, Manchester and Salford Methodist Mission, Wood Street Mission, A.J. Pass and Manchester Public Libraries for permission to reproduce some of the illustrations used in this book. I apologize in advance if I have overlooked anyone who should have been acknowledged and has not been.

I also wish to thank Simon Fletcher of Sutton Publishing for his help and also Sutton Publishing for giving me the opportunity to compile this collection of illustrations on Manchester. Without the work of publishers like Sutton Publishing illustrations of towns would not be so readily available, and many people would not have come to appreciate the historical importance of their own community.

Finally I would like to thank Peter and Anna, for the understanding that when their father is working on a new book he should not be disturbed any more than necessary, and my wife Hilary for her tolerance and encouragement while I have been working on this book, especially as I tend to spread out with books and papers everywhere.